THE EARLY CHILDHOOD
MENTORING CURRICULUM

Trainer's Guide

*

by

Dan Bellm

Marcy Whitebook

Patty Hnatiuk

Center for the Child Care Workforce

Washington, D.C.

Distributed to the general public by CCW.

Distributed to the trade by Gryphon House, Inc.
P.O. Box 207
Beltsville, MD 20704
telephone: (800) 638-0928
e-mail: orders@ghbooks.com

Printed in the U.S.A. by Harris Lithographics, Inc.

Book design: Elaine Joe

ISBN   1-889956-00-7 (*Handbook*)
       1-889956-01-5 (*Trainer's Guide*)

Center for the Child Care Workforce
733 15th Street, N.W., Suite 1037
Washington, D.C. 20005-2112
telephone: (202) 737-7700
fax: (202) 737-0370
e-mail: mentor@ccw.org

ACKNOWLEDGMENTS

The Early Childhood Mentoring Curriculum was made possible through the generous support of the Ewing Marion Kauffman Foundation and the Danforth Foundation. We would like to offer special thanks to Stacie Goffin, Steve Koon, Mike Helmer, Joy Torchia and Patty Mansur of the Kauffman Foundation, and to Wilma Wells of the Danforth Foundation, for their gracious help and guidance.

Many thanks also to the members of our Curriculum Advisory Board, who dedicated many hours to reviewing early drafts, and whose insight and expertise have strengthened this work immeasurably:

Betty Allen, Special Needs Resource Teacher, Eliot Pearson Children's School, Tufts University, Medford, Mass.

Pat Bolton, Family Child Care Provider, Westminster, Colo.

Diane Trister Dodge, President, Teaching Strategies, Inc., Washington, D.C.

Julie Olsen Edwards, Director, Early Childhood and Family Life Education Department, Cabrillo Community College, Aptos, Calif.

Nancy Johnson, Director, Child Care Works, Minneapolis, Minn.

Stephanie Johnson, Mentor Teacher, Associated Day Care Services, Boston, Mass.

Kathy Modigliani, Director, The Family Child Care Project, Center for Career Development, Wheelock College, Boston, Mass.

Peyton Nattinger, Director, California Early Childhood Mentor Program, Chabot College, Hayward, Calif.

An earlier version of The Early Childhood Mentoring Curriculum was developed for U.S. Army Child Development Services under Contract #MDA903-93-C-0250. Special thanks to Editorial Review Team members M.A. Lucas, Mary Ellen Pratt, Joy Guenther and Joe Perreault, who first helped bring this Curriculum to life.

We would also like to express our appreciation and gratitude to the many mentors, protégés and mentor program developers throughout the country whose groundbreaking efforts have contributed so much to the field of mentoring in early care and education.

The quotations from mentors which are interspersed throughout the *Handbook for Mentors* and *Trainer's Guide* are taken from *Mentoring in Early Care and Education: Refining An Emerging Career Path*, © 1994 Center for the Child Care Workforce.

The Center for the Child Care Workfroce (CCW), founded in 1978 as the Child Care Employee Project and known as the National Center for the Early Childhood Work Force from 1994 to 1997, is a nonprofit research, education and advocacy organization committed to improving child care quality by upgrading the compensation, working conditions and training of child care teachers and family child care providers. CCW coordinates the Early Childhood Mentoring Alliance, an information and technical assistance network for mentors and mentoring programs nationwide, and the Worthy Wage Campaign, a grassroots effort working for better-quality care for children and a better livelihood for teachers and providers.

In 1988, we co-founded the California Early Childhood Mentor Program, one of the earliest and largest early childhood mentoring efforts in the United States. We have produced several resource publications on mentoring, including an in-depth profile of mentoring programs nationwide.

Please write, phone or e-mail us to become a member of CCW, or to learn more about the Early Childhood Mentoring Alliance, the Worthy Wage Campaign, or our other publications and activities.

TABLE OF CONTENTS

Early care and education is an extremely diverse field, with young children being taught and cared for daily in such varied settings as child care centers, schools, and family child care homes. Our intended audience for The Early Childhood Mentoring Curriculum is the entire spectrum of the child care field, and in particular, we are eager to bridge the divide that has often separated center-based child care and family child care. While we have developed the Curriculum primarily for use in formal mentoring programs, it can also be used in a variety of child care classes and workshops, whether at community colleges, child care centers, family child care associations, Head Start agencies or other training and staff development programs.

How To Use These Materials

Ideally, trainers and mentors will have at least 30 to 40 hours of training time to work together before the mentoring process begins. The training model for the Early Childhood Mentoring Curriculum consists of a five-day mentoring course outline, in ten half-day modules, for covering the eight units (see page 99). These modules can be adapted to a variety of training schedules and situations.

The Curriculum is composed of two parts: this *Trainer's Guide*, and a *Handbook for Mentors*. The *Trainer's Guide* contains:

* goals and objectives for each of the eight Units in the *Handbook for Mentors*;

* suggested training activities, with handouts, for each Unit;

* a sample five-day mentoring course outline;

* a chapter on conducting effective group learning sessions; and

* a concluding chapter, with activities designed for the end of the mentor training course and the end of the mentors' work with their protégés.

The *Handbook for Mentors* is the primary text for the mentor training. It is designed not only as a resource for the trainer in covering the content areas of the eight Units, but as a handbook that the mentors will keep and use throughout their work with protégés. The *Handbook* contains:

* reading material for the trainer and the mentors on each of the eight Units;

* activities in each Unit that mentors can use, either on their own or with protégés;

* bibliographies in each Unit listing references and suggestions for further reading; and

* appendices with background information and resources.

Definitions of Terms

A mentor, historically and traditionally defined, is an older, more experienced person who is committed to helping a younger, less experienced person become prepared for all aspects of life (Odell, 1990).

Often used interchangeably with such terms as guiding, tutoring, coaching or counseling, "mentoring" can be a catch-all term to describe the relationship between a learned, skilled person and a novice.

In this Guide, we will use the term in a more specific sense, referring to teachers or providers who are concerned not only with how children grow and learn, but with helping other adults to become more effective practitioners. A "mentor" is an excellent teacher or provider who has worked in the field for a significant time and has received education and training in child development, early childhood education and the teaching of other adults.

Mentoring programs throughout the country vary in what they call the novice teacher or provider with whom a mentor works. Common terms include "protégé," "mentee," "apprentice" and "peer." Some prefer "protégé" because it refers to being guided and counseled by a more experienced colleague for the explicit purpose of furthering one's career. Similarly, "apprentice" focuses on the experiential learning of a trade under the tutelage of one who is already skilled in the work. "Mentee" is less formal but has yet to become widely accepted as a bona fide word. "Peer" is appealing because it emphasizes mutual learning and equality in the relationship. In this Guide we will primarily use the terms "mentor" and "protégé."[1]

The Importance of Mentoring Programs

While many of the mentoring concepts in the Early Childhood Mentoring Curriculum can be applied in various training environments, *mentoring*, to be truly effective, should have a formal structure. In particular, a mentoring program should provide mentors and protégés with the kinds of support that will allow them to work together freely—including release time from normal classroom or family child care home duties, and coverage of the classroom or home by qualified substitutes. To recognize their added level of work and professional responsibility, mentors should also receive additional compensation, and mentors and protégés, ideally, will receive college-level credit that can help them advance in the field. Finally, the mentoring relationship must be *voluntary*, with each partner agreeing on and understanding their mutual goals and expectations for the process.[2]

Participants in a mentoring program should also keep in mind that *the learning relationship flows both ways* between the mentor and protégé. Although the mentor is the more experienced early childhood practitioner, the protégé will no doubt have life experiences, cultural perspectives or areas of knowledge that the mentor can benefit and learn from, too. Mentors speak frequently of how much they learn in the process of helping other adults become better teachers and providers (Whitebook and Sakai, 1995):

My protégés always end up teaching me something new. I'm able to share my knowledge and experience with another teacher and also receive her knowledge and experience.

Teaching someone to teach makes you re-evaluate and improve your own methods.

Mentoring programs are based on the notion that experienced teachers and providers are more likely to stay in the field if they receive advanced education, salary enhancement, and the opportunity to share their expertise with novice caregivers and

---

1 For the sake of simplicity, we will also use feminine pronouns when discussing mentors and protégés, but we recognize that a significant number of men work in this predominantly female profession.

2 See Unit 2 for further discussion of how mentoring programs can be structured.

other colleagues. Mentoring programs reflect an understanding that professional development efforts must be directed at experienced as well as entry-level personnel, and must reward people for their efforts to further develop their skills. Both new and experienced caregivers benefit by becoming more *reflective* practitioners: that is, more able to examine and question their own practices.

Mentoring programs recognize that experienced teachers and providers have often been thrust informally into mentoring roles already—but without any recognition, training or compensation for this added work. Instead of a source of pride and accomplishment, this kind of unacknowledged, unsupported "mentoring" can easily become a source of frustration and resentment—in effect, an unpaid second job. In this labor-intensive field, our human capital is put to wisest use when excellent teachers and providers are trained and supported to pass on their expertise and professionalism to the next generation.

A variety of mentoring models have been developed in early care and education programs. Some establish mentor centers or family child care homes in the community for practicum students to visit. Some select teachers or providers who meet certain eligibility criteria to work with protégés either in their own classrooms or at their protégés' work places. Mentors can help protégés develop general caregiving skills or specialized skills in a particular area, such as small business management, working effectively with parents, setting up age-appropriate child care environments, or developing a curriculum. But whatever their structure, mentoring programs should be:

* responsive to the developmental needs of those they serve, and grounded in research on teacher and adult development;

* supportive in nature, rather than linked to formal personnel evaluation processes;

* forums for improving collegial connections between mentors, protégés, supervisors and trainers;

* learning systems that examine themselves, improve how they function, and contribute to the collective health of the early care and education community.

Equally important, mentor programs create a new step in the early childhood career progression, allowing a staff member or provider to advance professionally while continuing to educate and teach children directly. By creating a step in the career path that acknowledges the specialized skill of teaching others to care for and educate young children, and by combining this step with financial reward, mentor programs challenge the perception of child care as unskilled work. They also establish an incentive for adults to continue in the field, and by providing them with new opportunities for leadership, mentor programs strengthen the voice of practitioners in efforts to improve services for children and to enhance the professional growth of adults.

In her research on mentor teachers in K-12 settings, Joellen Killion (1990) has identified four significant outcomes for mentors:

1. *Growth.* In working with protégés, mentors are compelled to reflect on their own practice, and to examine their actions and beliefs about teaching. This inquiry, essential for professional development, helps mentors to define or refine their own educational philosophies.

2. *Recognition.* Selection as a mentor means recognition of accomplishment and sta-

tus. The role of mentor confers a certain "expert" designation, an acknowledgment that one has the qualities to make a significant contribution to the profession.

3. *Experience-enhancing roles.* The adoption of the mentoring role requires the acquisition of new knowledge and skills to assume new roles, whether as a resource specialist, consultant, facilitator, coach or other helper. Mentors become educational leaders who model effective personal and professional behaviors for other teachers, providers and colleagues.

4. *Collegiality.* By having the opportunity to meet with colleagues—either by welcoming others into their work environment, or by meeting with them in other settings—mentors facilitate collaboration and break the cycle of isolation in early childhood settings.

In supporting a new teacher or family child care provider, mentors:

* protect, sponsor, promote and "open doors";

* teach, coach, challenge, consult, advise and counsel;

* provide positive role models;

* problem-solve and move forward, leading others to more sophisticated stages of concern and cognitive development;

* guide their partners in practice along a path that enhances the potential for excellence in teaching.

Human growth is often caused by disequilibrium: the creative dissonance or tension between opposing ideas, approaches and points of view. Adults who are embarking on a period of creativity and growth, therefore, may frequently have a sense of being "off balance," "in over their heads" or "out on a limb." This is why it's important for mentoring programs to provide an environment in which adults feel safe to share and to take risks. Learning and growth can be enhanced by providing opportunities for role playing, by posing moral or practical dilemmas, by providing support and concrete feedback at times of challenge, and even by placing individuals in learning or teaching environments that are slightly more complex and demanding that the ones they would naturally prefer.

In essence, mentors generate and regenerate the process of learning—dealing critically and creatively with change that leads to transformation, in themselves and in the field. In our under-recognized, high-turnover profession, this is no small feat!

References

Killion, J.P. (1990). "The Benefits of An Induction Program for Experienced Teachers." *Journal of Staff Development*.

Odell, S.J. (1990). *Mentor Teacher Programs*. Washington, D.C.: National Education Association.

Whitebook, M., and Sakai, L. (1995). *The Potential of Mentoring: An Assessment of the California Early Childhood Mentor Program*. Washington, D.C.: Center for the Child Care Workforce.

Unit I

INTRODUCTION TO MENTORING

This introductory Unit discusses the value and purpose of mentoring, and defines some basic terms.

Goals and Objectives for Unit I

Upon completing this Unit, mentor trainees should be able to:

* define such terms as "mentoring," "mentor" and "protégé";

* discuss the goals of mentoring programs, and appreciate their importance for the child care field;

* understand the qualities of a good mentor.

The Activities in this Unit are designed to encourage mentor trainees to:

* recall their own experiences of being a new child care teacher or provider;

* discuss what a new teacher or provider might need from a mentor;

* reflect on their goals and expectations for the mentoring process;

* define for themselves "what makes a good mentor."

ACTIVITY 1-1

WHAT DOES MENTORING MEAN TO ME?
QUESTIONS FOR DISCUSSION

Purpose　　To serve as an introduction to basic mentoring concepts, and to reflect on one's own experiences, needs and goals in relation to mentoring.

Materials　　Large pad of newsprint, easel and markers, as well as small sheets of paper, and pencils or pens, if you wish to take notes from the discussions, and/or ask small groups to "report back" to the larger group.

Notes to Trainer　　Introduce one or more of the following topics as a springboard for *discussion* or *journal writing*.

Discussions of these questions can be held in small or large groups. If the class divides into small groups, reconvene as a large group before the session ends, to allow each small group to "report back" some of the high points of the discussion. (See also "Facilitating Discussions" on page 105.)

Alternatively, you can assign any of these questions to the mentor trainees as **journal-writing** exercises, which can then be shared or discussed later in class. (See the discussion of journal writing on page 37 of the *Handbook.*)

Time Required　　20-45 minutes for each of the six discussion topics, or 45-90 minutes for a session combining several of the topics.

*"I've known for a while that my self-esteem
increases when I can help other teachers, so I was very excited by the
opportunity to become a mentor. It's so stimulating and challenging.
Sometimes your mentee might not really like getting critical feedback, but it is
a special gift to learn how to be able to talk honestly with people about the
work they are doing."*

Topics for Activity 1-1

1. What did it feel like when you started your first job as a teacher or provider?

   ➤ What were your hopes, skills, strengths, needs, fears?

   ➤ How did you learn the skills you needed?

   ➤ Did anyone help you?

   ➤ What kinds of help were most valuable to you?

   ✳

2. Has anyone ever been a mentor to you (in a child care or other situation)? Consider parents and other family members, friends, co-workers at current or previous jobs and others in the community who have served as role models.

   ➤ What was the mentoring experience like?

   ➤ What did you most appreciate from that person?

   ➤ What did you learn?

   ✳

3. Have you ever been a mentor before, either in a child care situation or elsewhere?

   ➤ What did you do with or for another person?

   ➤ In what ways did you feel helpful or effective?

   ➤ In what ways might you like to become more helpful and effective as a mentor?

   ✳

4. What are the three most difficult challenges a new teacher or provider faces?

   ➤ What do new teachers or providers need to learn in order to do their jobs better?

   ➤ Did you receive help in these areas during your own first year in the field?

   ✳

5. What are your own personal goals for becoming a mentor?

   ➤ What are your three greatest strengths as a teacher or provider?

   ➤ Name three areas in which you need or want to learn more in order to do your job better.

   ✳

6. Think of something you do well (either related to working with children, or not), and imagine teaching this skill or concept to others.

   ➤ How would you do it?

   ➤ What would the steps be?

"I've been a family child care provider for twenty years.
By becoming a mentor, and responding to people's questions, I am realizing
how much I know. The more we can help other providers to do a good job,
the more we support ourselves and the community.**"**

ACTIVITY 1-2

WHAT MAKES A GOOD MENTOR?[1]

Purpose To identify the characteristics of good mentors and to discern which of these are the most important.

Materials Large pads of newsprint, easels, markers, small sheets of paper and pencils or pens.

Notes to Trainer As a background resource, consult the chart, "What Makes a Good Mentor?," on page 19 of the *Handbook*. If you wish, distribute copies of the chart at the end of the discussion—not to uphold it as containing "the right answers," but to validate what the group has said, to draw comparisons, and to discuss any differences or gaps between the group's discussion and the chart.

Time Required 30-45 minutes.

---

[1] Adapted with permission from Newton et al. (1994), "What Makes a Good Mentor?," 2-53.

Steps for Activity 1-2

1. Divide the class into small groups of four or five. Ask each group to identify a recorder who will write all responses on a sheet of newsprint.

   ✳

2. Ask each group to make a list of the characteristics which are important for being a good mentor (5-10 minutes).

   ✳

3. Ask each group to discuss its list and to identify the six most important characteristics (5-10 minutes).

   ✳

4. Reconvene as a large group, and ask each group to share its top six characteristics. Are there significant disagreements or differences, either within or among the small groups? Together, create a master list of "What Makes a Good Mentor," combining responses that are similar (15-20 minutes).

BECOMING A MENTOR: OPTIONS AND OPPORTUNITIES

This Unit builds on the introductory material in Unit 1 by discussing in greater detail the various ways in which mentoring programs can be structured.

Goals and Objectives for Unit 2

Upon completing this Unit, mentor trainees should be able to:

* anticipate the ways in which their job descriptions and professional roles may change as the result of becoming a mentor;

* understand the roles and responsibilities of a mentor and a protégé;

* distinguish between mentoring and supervision.

The Activities in this Unit are designed to encourage mentor trainees to:

* reflect on their own needs and desires for support during the mentoring process;

* use case examples to distinguish between mentoring and supervision;

* articulate a vision for the mentoring program.

ACTIVITY 2-1

WHAT KINDS OF SUPPORT DO I WANT?

Purpose   To reflect on one's needs for support as a mentor, and how a mentoring program might be designed to accommodate those needs.

Materials   Large pad of newsprint, easel, markers.

Notes to Trainer   See in particular the discussion of "Changes in the Job Descriptions and Professional Roles of Mentors" on page 24 of the *Handbook*. As mentors' jobs change, issues and/or possible misunderstandings could arise with co-workers, parents or directors. This activity can help mentors reflect in advance on how their jobs and working relationships might change, and what types of support they might need.

Time Required   30 minutes.

Steps for Activity 2-1

1. Ask mentors to describe the support systems or patterns they would find most helpful as they engage in their new mentoring roles. They should assume for the moment that resources are unlimited, so that they can feel free to describe ideal situations. Questions to consider include:

   ➤ Who should the support person(s) be, what are their roles and functions, and how often should they be available?

   ➤ Should the mentors themselves form a peer support group? How and when would they meet? In what ways could they help each other?

   ✳

2. Record all suggestions on a flip-chart.

   ✳

3. Discuss as a group which of these suggestions are the highest priorities. Whenever possible, incorporate these suggestions into the structure of the mentoring program.

"When I became a mentor, I had a chance to help others learn about small-business skills, and they helped me learn more about running a family day care. Knowing other providers and getting a chance to talk about what we do makes us feel much less isolated, and that's a big step towards improving the quality of care."

ACTIVITY 2-2

MENTORING VS. SUPERVISION

Purpose   To gain a practical understanding of the differences between mentoring and supervising.

Materials   Large pad of newsprint, easel and markers, if you wish to take notes from the discussion.

Notes to Trainer As background, consult the discussion of "The Differences Between Mentoring and Supervision" on page 26 of the *Handbook.*

Time Required   30-45 minutes.

Steps for Activity 2-2

Take the following (or other) scenarios, and lead a discussion which helps the mentor trainees sort out the differences between mentoring and supervising. Consider:

- → What could or should a mentor do in each situation?

- → What could or should a supervisor do?

- → What are the limits and opportunities in each role?

a. The protégé is consistently late for meetings, observations, or other agreed-upon activities.

b. The protégé does not complete paperwork or other agreed-upon tasks.

c. After observing the protégé in her classroom or home, you feel she needs more training or skill development in a particular area—e.g., setting up the play and learning environment; developing well-thought-out lesson plans; cultural sensitivity; or equal play and learning opportunities for boys and girls.

d. You observe the protégé yelling at or using sarcasm with children when she is impatient.

e. A child tells you—or you suspect—that the protégé has used physical punishment.

"Becoming a mentor is a another step in learning from each other. There is so little respect for this field, that we don't recognize what we know or have to offer. The Mentor Program has changed that—there is a new sense of professionalism and respect. I hope it will be realized by more and more people."

ACTIVITY 2-3

ARTICULATING A VISION OF THE MENTORING PROGRAM[1]

Purpose   To help develop a unified vision of the mentoring program, and to identify shared values and beliefs.

Materials   3"x5" index cards, in sufficient quantity for each trainee to have three cards, one for each of the questions below. Large pad of newsprint, easel and markers.

Notes to Trainer   This activity can empower mentor trainees to feel "invested" in the mentoring program early on, by asking them to help articulate the program's vision.

Time Required   Approximately 60 minutes.

---

1 Adapted with permission from Newton et al. (1994).

Steps for Activity 2-3

1. Pass out three index cards to each participant, and ask them individually to complete the following statements in writing, one per card.

The purpose of mentoring is to . . .

Mentoring is most successful when . . .

The result of our mentoring program will be . . .

　　　　✳

2. If you wish, ask participants to read aloud some of their responses to the three statements.

　　　　✳

3. Collect all the index cards, sorted into three sets. Then divide the class into three groups, each of which will be assigned one of the statements. Give each group the set of cards pertaining to their assigned statement.

　　　　✳

4. Ask each group to develop a revised statement that summarizes the variety of responses.

　　　　✳

5. Reconvene as a full group to read the full "vision statement." Make copies for everyone to keep as a reference.

BUILDING THE FOUNDATION FOR MENTORING: KEY AREAS OF KNOWLEDGE

In order to work with less experienced caregivers, mentors will naturally need to have a sound knowledge of the principles of child development and of good early childhood education practices. But in addition, there are five key areas of knowledge, backed up by theory and research, that are critical for teachers and providers to understand in order to be successful as mentors:

* adult development,

* reflective practice,

* culturally relevant anti-bias education,

* the process of change, and

* leadership and advocacy.

This Unit provides information about each of these areas of knowledge, except for leadership and advocacy, which is discussed in Unit 7.

Goals and Objectives for Unit 3

Upon completing this Unit, mentor trainees should be able to:

* appreciate some of the ways in which adult learners differ from, and are similar to, child learners;

* describe in basic terms the "phase" and "stage" theories of adult development;

* define and understand the importance of reflective practice;

* reflect on the nature, and value, of change in individuals and organizations.

In the area of anti-bias education, Louise Derman-Sparks has outlined the following basic goals for early childhood teachers and providers:[1]

* Increase their awareness of issues of gender, race, class, ethnicity, sexual preference and physical abilities—starting with themselves, with an understanding of and appreciation for their own origins, identities and attitudes.

* Learn to identify ways that biases affect them and their programs.

* Gain an understanding of how children develop identity and attitudes.

---

[1] Adapted with permission from Derman-Sparks (1989).

* Plan ways to introduce anti-bias curriculum into the setting.

The Activities in this Unit are designed to encourage mentor trainees to:

* apply theories of adult development to themselves and to the mentoring process;

* use journal writing and other tools to foster reflective practice in their own and their protégé' daily work;

* increase their awareness of diversity and bias, and respond actively to expressions of bias by adults and children;

* reflect on some of their own experiences of personal change.

ACTIVITY 3-1

ADULT DEVELOPMENT

Purpose To reflect on one's own personal history, and to construct a group "theory of adult development."

Materials Sufficient copies of the handout, "Adult Development: Three Theorists' Views," for each participant. Large pad of newsprint, easel and markers; paper, and pens or pencils.

Notes to Trainer A common dificulty in studying theories of adult development is that, confronted with theories developed by "experts," many students will feel that they have nothing to contribute, or have no knowledge of their own about adult development. But in order to benefit from theory, students have to be able to think critically about it. This activity can help de-mystify how theories are developed, and make the process less abstract.

Time Required 45-60 minutes.

"I had been teaching for thirteen years and felt it was time to leave the classroom. Part of it was the money, but I also felt I was losing my enthusiasm for the work. Then the Mentor Program came around and I decided to stay and give it a try. I realized that I was ready to teach adults as well as children, and the Mentor Program has opened up this whole new area for me. It has made me recommit to being a classroom teacher—not just for the children, but for the teachers. All of us mentors are working now to establish the role of mentor in our state certification system, to formalize the role so that long-term teachers can have a goal to move toward."

Steps for Activity 3-1

1. Ask each participant to write down, for each decade of their life thus far—0-10, teens, 20s, 30s, etc.—a list of one to three of the main concerns, tasks, or developmental challenges they had during that period. Use separate sheets of paper for each decade.

*

2. Set out all the papers for everyone to see, or ask participants to read what they've written so that the responses for each decade can be recorded on a flip-chart.

*

3. Ask the group to look at the lists for each decade and discuss the similarities and differences they find. What patterns emerge?

What overall patterns of progression or development do you see from one decade to the next?

*

4. Construct a rough decade-by-decade "developmental chart," using the group's list of tasks and challenges.

*

5. After this activity is complete, distribute the handout so that participants can compare the work of three prominent theorists with their own. Discuss differences and similarities between the group's developmental chart and what these theorists have to say. How would each locate herself within one of the theorists' models?

ADULT DEVELOPMENT (EARLY TO MIDDLE ADULTHOOD):
THREE THEORISTS' VIEWS

Theorist	Stages or phases of adult development	Key thoughts about the stages or phases of adult development
Erikson	Young adulthood (dominant conflict is intimacy versus isolation) Maturity (dominant conflict is generativity versus self-absorption) Old age (dominant conflict is integrity versus despair)	Stimulus for growth is psychological conflict. Successful resolution of psychological conflict at each phase results in specific capacity (i.e., resolution of intimacy versus isolation phase is the capacity to love; resolution of generativity versus self-absorption is the capacity to care; resolution of integrity versus despair phase is wisdom).
Gilligan	Level 1: Individual's primary concern is for one's own survival in the face of powerlessness. Level 2: Individual seeks goodness in caring for others and values self-sacrifice as the highest virtue. Level 3: Individual recognizes oneself as a legitimate object of care, and this insight becomes the framework for an ethic of care.	Two moral voices can be traced in describing problems involving moral conflict and choice: the voice of justice (equality) or the voice of care (attachment or connection). The two approaches constitute different ways of organizing a problem that lead to different reasoning strategies and different ways of thinking about what is happening and what to do. Moral orientation is associated with the sex of the reasoner (females focus on care, males focus on justice), the problem being solved, and the social class of the individual. Moral maturity entails an ability to see in at least two ways and speak in at least two languages—those of care and justice.
Kegan	Stage 1. Imperial balance: Persons at this stage orient to themselves and the world through their own needs; they do not have a shared reality. Stage 2. Interpersonal balance: Persons at this stage are inextricably tied to others for a sense of themselves; they avoid conflict and seek approval. Stage 3. Institutional balance: Persons at this stage can tolerate multiple views; their sense of self-control is a strength; personal achievements and responsibility are prominent; alternative strategies and mutual communication are prized. Stage 4. Interindividual balance: Person's individuality and interdependence are prominent; persons at this level have a high degree of autonomy and capacity for interdependence.	Growth unfolds through alternative periods of stability, instability, and temporary rebalance. Emphasis is on meaning, not just traits and behaviors that lie beneath behaviors. Opportunities and limits exist at every developmental point. Pain and exhilaration accompany transition as something is lost, but something is also gained.

Sources
Levine, S. *Promoting Adult Growth in Schools: The Promise of Professional Development* (1989).
Lieberman and Miller, eds., *Staff Development for Education in the 90s* (1991).
Gilligan et al., *Mapping the Moral Domain* (1988).

ACTIVITY 3-2

KEEPING A JOURNAL AS A TOOL FOR REFLECTION AND DIALOGUE[2]

Purpose To practice using journal-writing as a way to reflect on one's mentoring experience, and as a tool for dialogue with one's protégé.

Materials Copies of the handout, "Questions to Promote Reflection and Affirmations to Support Reflection," for each participant. Each participant should also have a journal/notebook, and pencils or pens.

Notes to Trainer See the discussion of journals on page 37 of the *Handbook*, which recommends that mentors keep a journal of their mentoring experience, and that they ask their protégé to keep a journal as well.

If the mentor training is taking place while mentors have already begun working with protégés, this activity can be adapted for writing about an issue that has arisen with one's protégé. Otherwise, trainees can write about a recent issue with a parent or co-worker. (Note that, depending on the composition of the group, trainees may be reticent to write about co-workers.)

Time Required 45-60 minutes.

---

[2] Adapted with permission from Newton et al. (1994).

Steps for Activity 3-2

1. Ask each participant to recall an important issue or problem that arose with a parent or co-worker in their child care setting during the past week, and to write about it in the journal, referring to the list of "Questions to Promote Reflection." Mention at the beginning that they will be asked to read (or summarize verbally) what they have written to a partner.

✳

2. Allow participants to write for 5-15 minutes.

✳

3. Divide into pairs. One partner in each pair should read or summarize verbally what she has written. Using the lists of "Questions" and "Affirmations," the pair should then discuss how, in the coming week, that person would like to address the issue she has written about. Then switch, allowing the other person to read or summarize her journal entry and discuss it with her partner. (10-15 minutes per partner).

✳

4. Reconvene as a large group to talk about this writing experience, allowing each pair to report back on the key points of their discussion. In what ways, if any, did writing about an issue help to clarify it?

Questions to Promote Reflection

- → Can you talk more about that?
- → Why do you think that happened?
- → What evidence do have about that?
- → What do you need?
- → What have you tried before?
- → Why did/didn't it work?
- → What does this remind you of?
- → What if it happened this way?
- → How else could you approach that?
- → What do you want to happen?
- → How could you do that?
- → When is the concern *most* pronounced?

Affirmations To Support Reflection

- → You can find a way that works for you when you are ready.
- → You can change if you want to.
- → You can grow at your own pace.
- → You can know what you need and ask for help.
- → You can experiment and explore. I will help you.
- → Your needs and reflections are important.
- → I like talking to you.

Adapted with permission from Newton et al. (1994).

ACTIVITY 3-3

CULTURAL INTROSPECTION[3]

Purpose   A discussion of the questions in this activity can help mentors begin a process of dialogue on diversity and bias by locating themselves within a cultural context. Mentors and protégés can also try this activity together to get to know each other better, and to understand and appreciate any cultural differences between them.

Materials   None.

Notes to Trainer   Issues of race, class and culture are often very loaded and difficult to talk about. As a result, this and the following two activities may require particularly strong facilitation on your part, since they ask participants to share sensitive material about themselves, and to listen carefully and respectfully to each other. See also "Facilitating Discussions" and "Tools for Effective Facilitation" on pages 105 and 106.

Time Required   45-60 minutes.

---

[3] Adapted with permission from Hidalgo (1993), "Multicultural Teacher Introspection," 101.

"Reflecting back to when I started in this field in 1985, I remember trying really hard to do my job well. I didn't have anyone from my background or culture who could be a role model I could follow. I struggled not only with the language but with the inexperience, and I didn't have an educational background. I was afraid of what people thought of me. I never asked any questions during or after any workshops or classes. It wasn't until a few years ago that I realized that I caught on to new ideas faster and easier by watching others and not by reading books."

Steps for Activity 3-3

1. Ask participants to divide into pairs. Ask each pair to take turns reflecting on their own family and cultural backgrounds, touching on such questions as:

   → Where were you born?

   → Where did you grow up?

   → How would you describe the neighborhood where you were raised?

   → What is your ethnic or racial heritage?

   → What languages or dialects were spoken in your home?

   → Was religion important during your upbringing? If yes, how?

   → Who makes up your family (either your family of origin, or the one you live with now)?

   → What traditions does your family follow?

   → What values does your family hold dear?

   → How do the members of your family relate to each other? For example, how is love expressed?

   → How is your culture expressed in your family?

   ✴

2. Reconvene as a large group to discuss these dialogues. What did participants learn about each other? What was most interesting, important, surprising, challenging? How might such a conversation be introduced into your relationship with your protégé?

ACTIVITY 3-4

TOPICS FOR RAISING CONSCIOUSNESS ABOUT DIVERSITY AND BIAS[4]

Purpose To help clarify participants' thoughts about cultural identity, and to identify discomforts and prejudices that could interfere with doing anti-bias work.

Materials None.

Notes to Trainer See note to Activity 3-3.

Time Required 45-60 minutes.

---

[4] Adapted with permission from Derman-Sparks
    (1989), "Getting Started: A Self-Education Guide."

Steps for Activity 3-4

1. Ask participants to divide into pairs. Discuss any of the following topics, or more than one in combination.

   ➤ Share how you describe or define your racial/ethnic identity. How do you feel about it? What's important, what's not? You may also want to include issues of gender, class, sexuality or physical ability.

   ➤ Share how you learned about these aspects of your identity. What are your earliest memories? What was fun or painful about what (or how) you learned about your identity?

   ➤ Share how you agree/disagree with your parents' views about race, ethnicity, gender, class, sexuality, physical ability, etc. If you disagree, how did you develop your own ideas? Who and what were significant influences on you? If you were or are a parent, what did you (or what do you want to) teach your own children?

   ➤ Write down a list of behaviors for boys and girls, or women and men, that you consider acceptable and unacceptable. Compare lists. Discuss what range of sex role behaviors you accept in the children in your program.

   ➤ Make a list of things you would want people to know about your racial and ethnic identity. Make another list of things you would *not* want people to say about your racial and ethnic identity.

   ✳

2. Reconvene as a large group to discuss these dialogues. What did participants learn about each other? What was most interesting, important, surprising, challenging? How might such a conversation be introduced into your relationship with your protégé?

Alternative or Follow-up Activity

Ask participants to write in their journals about any of the above topics, or more than one in combination. Then, in class, divide participants into pairs to discuss what they have written, and reconvene as a large group to discuss these dialogues.

ACTIVITY 3-5

RESPONDING TO DISCRIMINATORY REMARKS OR BEHAVIOR

Purpose To practice responses to inappropriate or hurtful remarks or behavior by adults or children.

Materials Copies of Handouts #1-3, "Case Examples," "Interrupting Discriminatory Behavior," and "Responding to Biased Remarks by Children," for all participants. Easel, newsprint, markers.

Notes to Trainer See note to Activity 3-3. Note that the handout, "Case Examples," contains examples of bias and discrimination between adults, between children, and between adults and children.

Time Required 45-60 minutes.

Steps for Activity 3-5

1. In small groups, discuss (or role play) any of the case examples in Handout #1, or others that group members can suggest from their experience. Propose appropriate responses.

*

2. As a large group, compare the small groups' responses to each case example, and record the results (both agreements and disagreements) on a large flip chart.

*

3. Read and review Handouts #2 and 3, "Interrupting Discriminatory Behavior" and "Responding to Biased Remarks by Children." Is there anything that group members would add or change in either list? Discuss ways that mentors and protégés can make it an ongoing, everyday part of their caregiving practices to respond immediately to discrimination or bias.

RESPONDING TO DISCRIMINATORY REMARKS OR BEHAVIOR: CASE EXAMPLES

1. During a morning observation of her protégé's classroom, a mentor notices that the protégé greets and speaks enthusiastically to parents whose first language is English, but does not speak to other parents whose first language is not English.

- What are some ways the mentor can respond to this observation with her protégé?

2. At a summer day camp for school-age children, a counselor observes a group of eight- and nine-year-old girls apparently teasing and rejecting another girl. The girl comes to the counselor crying, saying that the other girls called her "black" and "ugly." The camp is predominantly white, but the group includes two Latina girls and one who is bi-racial (African-American and white). The girl who is upset has recently come to the U.S. from the Caribbean. Her attire is different from the other girls (she tends to wear dresses, and bows in her hair), and she speaks with a Caribbean accent.

- How do you think the counselor might react? What should she do immediately? short-term? long-term?

3. During large motor play outdoors, just before the morning circle time is about to begin, an African-American female teacher observes a group of preschool children chasing and playfully taunting each other. But to her dismay, some of the children are pulling at the corners of their eyes and shouting "Chinese eyes!" The center is diverse, with African-American, Latino and white children enrolled, but there are currently no Asian-American children. The only Asian-American at the center is a male work-study student of Japanese descent.

- How might the teacher react? What should she do immediately? short-term? long-term?

4. One of the four-year-old boys in a family child care program loves to play in the dress-up corner, and he is especially drawn to wearing the women's dresses, hats and shoes. The provider and the other children cheerfully accept this behavior as a normal kind of dramatic play, but the provider begins to overhear a couple of the parents making comments to each other about this child—calling him female names, for example, or "wondering whether he is a boy or a girl." They appear to be embarrassed and offended by the boy's behavior.

- How might the provider react? What should she do immediately? short-term? long-term?

5. During a post-observation conference, an African-American protégé complains to her mentor, "The lead teacher never allows me to lead group time, but she lets white student teachers from the local college take right over every week. I don't think she believes I'm capable, but I am!"

- How can the mentor respond to this?

6. A group of children is getting ready to go outside. Teacher/provider #1 (an African-American female) is trying to get the children to line up with their assigned partners. Fred, who is white, has been assigned to be partners with Joe, who is African-American. Teacher/provider #2 (a Latina female) is waiting with the other children, and hears the following interchange:

Teacher/provider #1: Fred and Joe, please line up. You two are partners.

    Fred: I don't want to be his partner. I don't like him.

     Joe: Well, I don't like you either. You're stupid.

    Fred: I'm not! You're black!

Teacher/provider #1: O.K., that's enough. You two change partners!

- How might teacher/provider #2 respond—immediately? short-term? long-term?

INTERRUPTING DISCRIMINATORY BEHAVIOR

1. **Don't ignore it.** Do not let an incident pass without remark. To do so gives the message that you are in agreement with such behavior or attitudes. If the intervention would jeopardize anyone's safety, it should not take place at the exact time or place of the incident, but it must be brought up as soon as appropriate.

2. **Explain and engage when raising issues.** Avoid preaching or being self-righteous.

3. **Don't be afraid of possible tension or conflict.** In certain situations this may be unavoidable. These are sensitive and deep-seated issues that won't change without some struggle. Try to model for children and co-workers that constructive conflict can be positive and resolved.

4. **Be aware of your own attitudes, stereotypes and expectations, and be open to discovering the limitations they place on your perspective.** We are all victims of our misconceptions to some degree, and none of us remain untouched by the discriminatory images and behaviors we have been socialized to accept.

5. **Project a feeling of understanding and forgiveness when events occur.** Don't assign guilt or blame.

6. **Recognize that you may become frustrated.** Discriminatory behavior won't be eradicated in a day or from one "multicultural presentation." Sometimes things may seem to get worse before they get better. This is a constant process of change and growth, even in a supportive environment.

7. **Be aware of your own hesitancies to intervene in these situations.** Be willing to examine your own fears about interrupting discrimination.

8. **Be a role model.** In everything you do with children and adults, reflect and practice the positive values you are tying to teach.

9. **Be non-judgmental but know the bottom line.** Issues of human dignity and equality are non-negotiable.

10. **Distinguish between categorical thinking and stereotyping.** For example, "redheads" is a category, but "redheads have fiery tempers" is a stereotype.

Adapted with permission from Guidice and Wortis (1987).

RESPONDING TO BIASED REMARKS BY CHILDREN

Adults often feel uncomfortable about responding to insulting or biased remarks that children make. There is no easy solution; what is required of an adult is to listen carefully, assess the remark, and respond thoughtfully, appropriately and immediately. When responding to such remarks, keep the following guidelines in mind. In most situations, all of the guidelines will be appropriate when used in this order.

1. **Acknowledge** that you heard an insulting remark.

2. **Offer support** to the child who has been insulted.

3. **Make clear** to the children that such remarks are not acceptable, but without judging or insulting the child who made the remark.

4. **Identify** what was inappropriate and/or hurtful about the remark.

5. **Correct** any misinformation carried or implied by the remark.

6. **Be sure** also, if it is appropriate, to help the children resolve any part of their conflict which has nothing to do with race or culture.

Adapted from Council on Interracial Books for Children, and Multicultural Project for Communication and Education (1984).

ACTIVITY 3-6

CHANGE BEGINS WITH EACH OF US[5]

Purpose To familiarize participants with the nature of change around us and to consider how we all deal with it personally.

Materials Enough copies of the handout, "Stages of Change," for each participant; journals; newsprint, easels, markers, blank paper, and pencils or pens.

Notes to Trainer This activity is designed to demonstrate that we all know more about the change process than we realize. Change occurs naturally. Resistance to change and efforts to maintain the status quo are natural reactions that can be anticipated. Be sure to note to participants at the outset that they will be asked to write in their journal, and to read (or summarize verbally) what they have written to one other person.

Time Required 45-60 minutes.

---

[5] Adapted with permission from Newton et al. (1994).

Steps for Activity 3-6

1. Review the discussion of "The Process of Change" in Unit 3 of the *Handbook*.

   ✳

2. Ask participants to individually make a list of three personal changes that they have undergone in the last year (for example, a change in a relationship; a new job, car, home, apartment, baby or pet; a new routine, pattern or hobby; or physical changes in weight, appearance or health). (2-5 minutes).

   ✳

3. Ask participants to choose one of these— preferably a personal change that has influenced their professional practice—and write about it in their journals. (The more powerful the example they select, the

more worthwhile the activity.) Ask them to describe the process of change that took place, any stages of adjustment they went through, and where they are now in the progression. (10-15 minutes).

   ✳

4. Divide the group into pairs. Ask participants to read their journal entries (or summarize them verbally) to their partner, and to look for common themes and/or notable differences in their anecdotes. (10-15 minutes).

   ✳

5. As a large group, discuss what implications these experiences of change might have for our work as mentors. List ideas on newsprint. (10-15 minutes).

GROWING AND DEVELOPING AS A TEACHER OR PROVIDER

This Unit builds on the discussion of adult development in Unit 3 to focus on the professional growth and development of teachers and providers, with particular reference to the work of Dr. Lilian Katz.

Goals and Objectives for Unit 4

Upon completing this Unit, mentor trainees should be able to:

* describe the most commonly identified developmental stages of child care teachers and providers;

* apply this theoretical information to mentoring relationships;

* discuss the needs of beginning teachers and providers;

* understand the qualities of experienced and effective teachers and providers.

The Activities in this Unit are designed to encourage mentor trainees to:

* assess their own developmental stages as teachers or providers;

* reflect on experiences, people and events that have contributed to their professional growth.

ACTIVITY 4-1

DEVELOPMENTAL STAGES

Purpose To reflect on one's own stage of professional development as a teacher or provider, using a prominent theorist's model as a resource.

Materials Copies of Appendix 1 of the *Handbook*, "Teachers' Developmental Stages." Journals/notebooks for each participant. Large pad of newsprint, easel and markers, if you wish to take notes from the discussion in Step #4.

Notes to Trainer Be sure to tell participants at the outset that they will be asked to write in their journal, and to read (or summarize verbally) what they have written to one other person.

Time Required 45-60 minutes.

"I am a toddler teacher but I never intended to teach lower than third grade. I decided to stick with my job until I could get one in the public school. After three years I finally began to feel comfortable about what I was doing. If I'd had a mentor, if someone had helped me learn what I needed to know to care for kids at this age, it would have been so much easier and more fun. I get a lot of satisfaction as a mentor, helping others get started. My own teaching is improving as I think about what I am doing and why. Now I'm not waiting for a "real" teaching job. I am in child care, and I know I am already working in the field of education.**"**

Steps for Activity 4-1

1. Before the class session, ask mentors to read the article, "Teachers' Developmental Stages," by Lilian G. Katz, in Appendix 1 of the *Handbook*. Review and discuss it briefly.

*

2. Ask each participant to write a brief assessment of their own stage of professional development. What are the characteristics of this stage? Which developmental hurdles have you already passed? What are the main challenges that now lie ahead for you? Would you revise Katz's four-stage model in any way, if it does not seem to apply closely enough to your own experience? (10-15 minutes).

*

3. Divide the group into pairs, and ask everyone to read (or summarize verbally) what they have written to their partner. Each pair should discuss common themes and/or differences. (15 minutes).

*

4. Reconvene as a large group to discuss these conversations. What did participants learn about each other? What was most interesting, important, surprising, challenging? How might such a conversation be introduced into your relationship with your protégé? (15-20 minutes).

Alternative Activity

1. Ask mentors to think of a teacher or provider with whom they have worked, and to briefly describe in writing the characteristics or behaviors of that person.

*

2. Using Katz's four stages of development, ask participants to identify which stage most accurately describes their colleague.

*

3. Ask participants to divide into pairs or small groups of 3-4 people, read (or summarize verbally) their description of the colleague, and tell their reasons for categorizing that person into a certain developmental stage. What would be appropriate supports and challenges for a teacher/provider at this stage?

*

4. Reconvene as a large group to discuss these conversations

Follow-up Activity

Ask mentors to conduct a similar self-assessment with their protégés, either in an informal discussion or in writing, using the Katz article as a resource. Are there any significant differences in the ways the mentor and the protégé assess the protégé's level of development? If so, what do these differences reveal? What steps need to be taken so that the mentor and protégé can reach agreement on their goals for the mentoring relationship?

ACTIVITY 4-2

A DEVELOPMENTAL SEQUENCE OF CAREGIVING BEHAVIORS[1]

Purpose   To present another view of the progression of development in adults.

Materials   Enough copies (on heavy card stock) of the handout, "Caregiving Behaviors," cut up into squares and placed in envelopes, for small groups of four to six participants. Prepare enough card sets and envelopes so that each group will have one.

Notes to Trainer   There is by no means one "right way" to order these descriptions of caregiving behaviors into a developmental sequence. Some behaviors may occur at a variety of developmental stages, or mean different things at different times. The variety of ways that a group can order these cards is one of the most interesting aspects of the activity.

Time Required   30-45 minutes.

---

[1] Adapted with permission from Newton et al. (1994).

Steps for Activity 4-2

1. Ask mentors to form small groups of four to six, and have each group identify a reporter.

*

2. Ask each small group to order the descriptions of caregiver behaviors in its envelope into clusters of similarity that make sense to the group.

*

3. Ask the groups then to order these clusters into developmental progressions that make sense to them.

*

4. Reconvene as a large group, and have the reporter for each group share the group's rationale for clustering and ordering the descriptions of behavior.

*

5. Discuss any differences in perspective among the small groups, and attempt to reach consensus about ordering the descriptions of behavior into one continuum of development. Be sure to allow for well-defended differences of opinion.

Unwilling to take advice	Continually asks for advice and/or affirmation on performance in classroom or child care home	Takes limited risks in caregiving approaches
Conforms with the majority in most cases	Shares new knowledge with colleagues	Incorporates research findings and information on good practice into her work
Helps others "grow"; not disparaging but supportive of others "behind" her	Has a good sense of classroom/home climate and of relationships among children; is sensitive to subtle changes and responds in the moment	Is able to recognize and use "teachable moments"
Develops and offers activities that are well planned so they flow smoothly, creates orderly environment	Seeks and listens to feedback from parents, children, colleagues, etc.	Seeks professional growth opportunities
Tends to accept ideas from others more rapidly than her own	Enforces discipline through cajoling and bargaining rather than clearly defined and consistently enforced expectations	Accepts any suggestions unquestioningly
Doesn't voice professional opinion	Refers classroom "challenges" to director excessively	Accepts ideas only from perceived "experts" or people who have authority over her
Tends to be overly critical of self and/or others	Interested in knowing about what children have learned, experienced and done in broader context than classroom or child care program	Has a clear idea of which rules are the most important; weeds out nonessentials
Shows interest in how children arrive at decisions and answers; not necessarily just interested in "right" answer	Begins to gain perspective on her place in the profession as a whole	Has achieved personal/professional balance

"_After seven years of teaching, I was at a crossroads._
I didn't really want to leave my classroom, but I kept thinking about what I
should do next. I needed a new challenge. Becoming a mentor teacher re-
energized me—I was able to learn more about myself as a teacher, and I
have learned a lot from my student. I feel so much better about myself and
what I can contribute.**"**

ACTIVITY 4-3

QUESTIONS FOR DISCUSSION

Purpose   To reflect on one's own development as a teacher or provider.

Materials   Large pad of newsprint, easel, markers, small sheets of paper, and pencils or pens, if you wish to take notes from the discussions, and/or ask small groups to "report back" to the larger group.

Notes to Trainer   Introduce one or more of the following topics as a springboard for *discussion* or *journal writing*.

Discussions of these questions can be held in small or large groups. If the class divides into small groups, reconvene as a large group before the session ends, to allow each small group to "report back" some of the high points of the discussion. (See also "Facilitating Discussions" on page 105.)

Alternatively, you can assign any of these questions to the mentor trainees as *journal-writing* exercises, which can then be shared or discussed later in class. (See the discussion of journal writing on page 37 of the *Handbook*.)

Time Required   20-45 minutes for each of the four discussion topics, or 45-90 minutes for a session combining several of the topics.

Topics for Activity 4-3

1. **Turning Points.** Think about your journey as a teacher or provider: where you started, the various roles you have played, and how you have grown. What turning points have you faced? Reflect on those places in your journey where you came to a "fork in the road" and had to make a choice. Select one of these "turning point" experiences to think about in detail. What did you learn from the experience? Who was with you on that "road?" How did others contribute to the insights you gleaned from the experience? How has the experience left its mark on you as a teacher or provider?

*

2. **Peak Experiences.** Reflect on the "peak experiences" you have had in professional development—high points that have particularly contributed to your growth. Select one to think about in detail. What was the experience and how did you become involved? Were others part of the experience? What role did they play? How did the experience influence your thinking about what is important in caring for young children? What insights did you gain? How have those insights influenced choices you have made since then? What symbol might capture the essence of the experience and what it taught you?

*

3. **Risks.** What risks have you taken as a teacher or provider in your quest to enhance your own teaching and learning? Select one risk experience—big or small —that really paid off or taught you something important. What did you do? How did you feel? What did you learn from the experience?

*

4. **Leaders.** Reflect on individuals you admire as leaders—in the world, in your community, in the child care field, or in

your own home or work place. They might be well known or relatively unknown. Then select one leader you particularly respect to think about in detail. Why do you respect this person so much? What special qualities does this person exhibit? How does this person affect the lives of others? How has this person shaped your beliefs about leadership, or about your own role as a leader? What do you believe are the three most important qualities a leader should possess, and why?

*

After any or all of these discussions, ask the small groups to list common themes, beliefs or values that are reflected in their personal stories. What are the commonalties among us? What are the differences?

BUILDING RELATIONSHIPS
BETWEEN MENTORS AND PROTÉGÉS

Through modeling and instruction, you can help mentors develop the skills they need to build good relationships with their protégés. Building a strong relationship depends not only on interpersonal skills but on self-awareness. As a result, your primary role in this area may be to help mentors recognize the individual strengths, weaknesses, beliefs and attitudes that help or hinder their communication and relationships with others.

Real or perceived differences also play an important role in the way we read and judge other people. Differences in age, gender, ability, culture, language, race, religion, sexual orientation, political beliefs, socioeconomic status and national origin can stand in the way of understanding, communicating and building relationships. (See the discussions of "Respect for Diversity in Early Childhood Settings" and "Guiding Principles for Anti-Bias Education in Mentoring" in Unit 3 of the *Handbook*). Through discussion, you can help mentors become more aware of their own, often unconscious, assumptions about differences, and how they constrain their thinking and conclusions about others. The result will be a better climate for fostering relationships.

Goals and Objectives for Unit 5

Upon completing this Unit, mentor trainees should be able to:

* recognize the importance of self-awareness, and respect for differences, in building trusting relationships with others;

* review the roles of responsibilities of mentors and protégés, first discussed in Unit 2;

* establish expectations and set goals with a protégé;

* identify their protégés', and their own, needs for support;

* understand the various stages which a relationship between a mentor and a protégé might undergo.

The Activities in this Unit are designed to encourage mentor trainees to:

* practice ways to establish expectations with a protégé for the mentoring relationship;

* assess the quality of their relationships with their protégés.

ACTIVITY 5-1

ESTABLISHING EXPECTATIONS

Purpose   To reflect upon, and create a statement about, expectations for a mentoring relationship.

Materials   Copies of the handout, "Mentors' Expectations for the Mentoring Relationship," for each participant; paper; and pencils or pens.

Notes to Trainer   Participants may wish to adapt or revise the handout, rather than creating their own from scratch.

Time Required   60 minutes.

"I *was looking forward to having a mentee but I didn't realize what I would learn from her. My mentee was one of those people who sees the shining light in the most challenging child. It really helped me to see some of the children differently through her eyes. I have been given at least as much as I have received.***"***

Steps for Activity 5-1

1. In a large group, discuss why it is important to be clear about one's expectations for a mentoring relationship.

    ✳

2. Read the handout.

    ✳

3. In small groups, discuss reactions to the handout, based on one's own experiences of relationships in which expectations have or have not been clear.

    ✳

4. Ask each small group to draft a list of expectations they have for a mentoring relationship. What are the essential components of such a relationship? Each small group should assign a reporter who can report back to the large group.

    ✳

5. In the large group, ask participants to share their lists of expectations, and discuss ways that mentors and protégés can clarify their expectations to each other.

MENTORS' EXPECTATIONS FOR THE MENTORING RELATIONSHIP

As your mentor:

- I will be available to you.

- I will help, support and encourage you in managing your work load, and setting up routines.

- We will work together to solve problems related to your caregiving career that are important to each of us.

- We will treat each other with respect, for example, by keeping appointments, completing assignments, and meeting other agreed-upon expectations.

- I will observe your interactions with children and provide you with feedback that will help inform your teaching practice.

- Although I do not have "all the answers," I will help you frame the questions that will lead you to your own answers and questions.

- I will share with you and demonstrate what I have learned about working with young children.

- I will treat everything that occurs in our mentoring relationship with confidentiality.

- We will learn from and with each other.

- I will not interfere with your relationships with your supervisor or clients.

Source: Adapted with permission from Saphier, J. and R. Gowner (1987), *The Skillful Teacher: Building Your Teaching Skills*. Carlisle, MA: Research for Better Teaching.

ACTIVITY 5-2

TAKING THE PULSE OF YOUR MENTORING RELATIONSHIP[1]

Purpose   To help mentors reflect on important aspects of their relationship with a protégé.

Materials   Sufficient copies of the handout, "Taking the Pulse of Your Relationship: A Checklist for Mentors." Paper, and pens or pencils.

Notes to Trainer   This activity can be used as a form of self-assessment for mentors at the beginning of, and throughout, their mentoring experience. The checklist can be used privately by the mentor as a personal tool, or voluntarily shared with others in discussion.

Time Required   5-10 minutes to fill out checklist; 20-45 minutes for discussion.

---

[1] Adapted, with permission, from Newton et al. (1994).

Steps for Activity 5-2

1. Introduce the handout as a tool that can help the mentor reflect upon her behaviors, actions, and attitudes in any given mentoring relationship.

✳

2. Ask mentors to complete the checklist and to think about a specific example for each item on the checklist. If the mentors are not already working with protégés, ask them to use the checklist—as much as it is applicable—to reflect on their relationship with another colleague.

✳

3. In small groups, ask participants to share examples of behaviors for each item. Each group should assign a recorder who can report back to the large group.

✳

4. In the large group, each small group can share some of their most interesting, surprising or challenging examples.

TAKING THE PULSE OF YOUR RELATIONSHIP: A CHECKLIST FOR MENTORS

❑ **N = never**   ❑ **S = sometimes**   ❑ **F = frequently**   ❑ **A = always**

N S F A

❑ ❑ ❑ ❑   I accept my protégé as a unique individual.

❑ ❑ ❑ ❑   I help my protégé feel she belongs in the program and in the profession.

❑ ❑ ❑ ❑   I show confidence in my protégé.

❑ ❑ ❑ ❑   I let my protégé know I care about her.

❑ ❑ ❑ ❑   I make my protégé feel she has something to contribute.

❑ ❑ ❑ ❑   I sense that my protégé is comfortable bringing problems to me.

❑ ❑ ❑ ❑   I let my protégé express her feelings and ideas.

❑ ❑ ❑ ❑   When I meet with my protégé, I listen more than I speak.

❑ ❑ ❑ ❑   I live up to the agreements we have made.

❑ ❑ ❑ ❑   I keep information about my protégé confidential.

❑ ❑ ❑ ❑   I provide her with resources for developing constructive ideas.

❑ ❑ ❑ ❑   I offer constructive feedback based on observational data.

❑ ❑ ❑ ❑   I respectfully and actively listen to and consider her point of view.

❑ ❑ ❑ ❑   I continually seek to improve my ability to assess others in a just and impartial way.

❑ ❑ ❑ ❑   I refrain from negative comments and making misinformed judgments about others.

❑ ❑ ❑ ❑   I treat my protégé without prejudice.

❑ ❑ ❑ ❑   I continually seek to improve my professional and interpersonal skills.

❑ ❑ ❑ ❑   I model self-reflection.

❑ ❑ ❑ ❑   I nurture my protégé's self-reflection.

❑ ❑ ❑ ❑   I volunteer my special skills.

❑ ❑ ❑ ❑   I am proud of my profession.

❑ ❑ ❑ ❑   I evaluate the attitudes and activities of my protégé with an open mind.

❑ ❑ ❑ ❑   I encourage the personal and professional growth of my protégé.

❑ ❑ ❑ ❑   I am kind and tolerant.

❑ ❑ ❑ ❑   I feel competent to help my protégé in the areas where it is most needed.

❑ ❑ ❑ ❑   I help my protégé identify her strengths and build upon them in new or difficult situations.

❑ ❑ ❑ ❑   I respect my protégé's supervisory line, and her relationships with client families.

Adapted with permission from Newton et al. (1994), "Taking the Pulse on Your Relationship: A Checklist for Mentors," 3-67 to 3-68.

Unit 6

SKILLS FOR EFFECTIVE MENTORING

This Unit discusses the following sets of interpersonal skills that are essential for effective mentoring:

* communication

* modeling

* giving and receiving feedback

* observation, coaching and conferencing

* self-assessment

* resolving conflict

* avoiding burnout.

Giving and receiving critical feedback, and resolving conflicts, are perhaps the hardest things for mentors and protégés to do—especially for people who are accustomed to unsupportive supervision, or who have often received feedback in negative ways. Practicing these skills in role plays and in real-life situations should therefore be an important focus when teaching this Unit.

Goals and Objectives for Unit 6

Upon completing this Unit, mentor trainees should be able to:

* define the concept of *disposition* toward their work with children and adults;

* understand and practice a variety of *communication* skills;

* demonstrate good caregiving practices to a protégé through *modeling*;

* give and receive *constructive feedback* to/from a protégé;

* conduct an *observation and conferencing* process;

* utilize a *self-assessment* tool;

* understand and practice a model of *conflict resolution*;

* appreciate the seriousness of *burnout* in the child care profession, and take steps to avoid undue stress.

The Activities in this Unit are designed to encourage mentor trainees to:

* practice the communication skill of "active listening";

* experience an observation and conferencing process;

* identify and resolve conflict;

* assess sources of stress, and potential causes of burnout, in their work environment.

ACTIVITY 6-1

ACTIVE LISTENING[1]

Purpose   To practice the art of "active listening" with a partner, and/ or as a large group.

Materials   Copies of the handout, "Active Listening," for all participants. Large pad of newsprint, easel and markers, if you wish to take notes from the large group discussion in step #4.

Notes to Trainer   See the discussion of active listening in the discussion of "Communication," on page 78 of the *Handbook*. Step #5 (asking participants to role-play a conversation in front of the whole group) could require some assertive facilitation on your part—for example, being willing to gently interrupt the role play to make suggestions, if the participants are not modeling "active listening" very clearly, and then asking them to continue.

Time Required   30-60 minutes.

---

[1] Adapted with permission from Newton et al. (1994).

Steps for Activity 6-1

1. Review and discuss the handout.

    *

2. Divide the group into pairs. One partner in each pair should describe a difficulty that she is having in her child care program, including:

    → a description of the situation;

    → why she is having trouble with it; and

    → any details about the roles of other people who may be connected to the problem.

    The other person in the pair is the "active listener," who should let her partner know she is being heard by means of body language, responsive comments and constructive feedback about the situation. Each pair should then switch roles, so that each person has an opportunity to be a speaker and a listener. (5-10 minutes per partner.)

    *

3. Each pair should take a few minutes to discuss this experience with each other. What worked well, or didn't? How did the conversation feel?

    *

4. In a large group discussion, ask participants to describe this experience. In what ways—through what signals, or behavior—did they feel heard or not heard by their partner?

    *

5. Alternatively, or in addition, one or more of these conversations could be conducted in front of the whole group, after which the group members can offer constructive feedback about what they observed.

HANDOUT FOR ACTIVITY 6-1
ACTIVE LISTENING

Requires: attention, with congruent body language
acknowledgment
paraphrasing
summarizing

Allows others to: suggest solutions to be tried
form their own interpretations
draw their own inferences

"Each week we talk about classroom experiences,
concerns or questions, my protégé's classroom experience, what is working
and what is not, specific children, parent interactions, and staff relationships.
We try to keep a handle on balance and how to avoid burnout. Respect is the
key. I respect my protégé's ability to know herself and to know what she is
ready for. I can gently challenge her, but she is the only one who can
determine whether the challenge is accepted."

ACTIVITY 6-2

OBSERVATION, COACHING AND CONFERENCING

Purpose   To practice coaching and conferencing techniques.

Materials   Copies of the handout, "Classroom Observation: A Case Example." Large pad of newsprint, easel and markers, if you wish to take notes from the group discussion.

Notes to Trainer   You may also wish to generate other case scenarios for the group to work with, or invite participants to suggest scenarios from their own experience. Also see "Questions to Promote Reflection" and "Affirmations to Support Reflection," the handout for Activity 3-2.

Time Required   30-45 minutes.

Steps for Activity 6-2

1. Ask participants to read the handout, and to imagine that they are Mary's mentor and have just observed this activity.

*

2. In small groups, or all together, discuss ways of working with Mary in a post-observation conference. What questions can you ask that will help her reflect on the activity, rather than making her feel criticized or defensive? (Examples: What did you plan? How do you feel it worked? How did it differ from what you planned? How would you do it differently next time?) What kinds of feedback or questions would not be helpful?

*

3. If you have broken up into small groups, reconvene as a large group to compare notes.

CLASSROOM OBSERVATION: A CASE EXAMPLE

The setting is a classroom for four-year-olds at a child care center. At the end of a long circle time in a large group, the children move to small groups for "work time." One teacher, Mary, has six children in her group. She immediately captures their attention by holding up a plastic bag filled with hand puppets with velcro attachments. (One has five monkeys attached to the glove; another has five pumpkins, etc.) But for several frustrating minutes—for her and the children—Mary tries to get everyone to sit quietly so that she can begin the activity, which consists of each child, one by one, selecting a puppet and choosing a song to sing.

The first child picks the monkey puppet and sings, "Five little monkeys jumping on the bed...." But by the time the child gets to the third monkey in the song, the other children are grabbing at her puppet and at the other puppets resting by Mary's knee. They are having a very difficult time waiting for their turn.

Mary does not pass out the other puppets, or let the group share the puppet that is currently in use. Instead, she continues in the same manner for another ten minutes, with the children wiggling, distracted and barely engaged in the singing because they are so focused on wanting to touch the puppets. Two children try to walk away from the activity completely. Mary repeatedly stops the activity to remind the children of the rules, and by the end she seems cross and exhausted.

ACTIVITY 6-3

CONFLICT ROLE-PLAYS

Purpose   To practice resolving potential conflicts that could arise between a mentor and a protégé.

Materials   Copies of handout, "Rules for Constructive Controversy," for each participant. Large pad of newsprint, easel and markers, if you wish to take notes from the group's feedback on the role plays.

Notes to Trainer   If the participants would feel more comfortable doing so, pairs could practice role plays in front of small groups, rather than the entire group. In this case, the large group should re-gather at the end to hear about each other's experiences. Alternatively, participants could do the role plays by themselves in pairs, and then return to the large group to discuss them.

Time Required   30-60 minutes.

Steps for Activity 6-3

1. Review the handout, "Rules for Constructive Controversy."

✳

2. Ask for pairs of volunteers to role-play any of the following situations between a mentor and a protégé (5-10 minutes each):

  → A protégé who feels intimidated by her mentor's personal style, or by her greater level of experience and skill, and a mentor who does not understand why the protégé seems so unwilling to benefit from what she has to offer.

  → A mentor who observes her protégé behaving harshly toward a child, and experiences internal conflict about how to challenge the protégé in a positive and helpful way, without embarrassing or alienating her.

  → A protégé who is resistant to receiving any kind of challenging feedback from her mentor.

  → A protégé who believes that the mentor is insensitive to cultural differences among children, but is afraid to raise the issue because she views the mentor as "the expert."

  Participants should also be welcome to suggest their own ideas for role plays.

✳

3. At the end of each role play, enlist the large group's help in proposing solutions or ways to respond.

RULES FOR CONSTRUCTIVE CONTROVERSY

1. Focus on achieving the goal, not on dominating the other person.

2. Take active part in discussions.

3. Value, respect and take seriously the other person's contribution.

4. Be critical of ideas, not of individuals.

5. Strive to understand the position and frame of reference of those with whom you disagree.

6. Bring out differences of opinion and then combine several positions into a creative solution.

7. Argue rationally: generate ideas, organize reasons and draw conclusions.

8. Evaluate contributions based on soundness, not on who proposed them.

In constructive controversy:

➤ Relationships are stronger.

➤ People who have experienced conflict like and trust each other more.

➤ Both parties are satisfied with the results of the conflict.

➤ Both parties have improved their ability to resolve future conflicts with one another.

Adapted with permission from Newton et al. (1994).

ACTIVITY 6-4

STRESS IN THE CHILD CARE WORK ENVIRONMENT

Purpose To reflect on, and address, some of the causes of stress or burnout in the child care work environment.

Materials Large pad of newsprint, easel and markers for large group; paper, and pens or pencils, for small groups.

Notes to Trainer For background, see the discussion of "Avoiding Burnout" on page 86 of the *Handbook*.

Time Required 30-60 minutes.

Steps for Activity 6-4

1. Divide participants in small groups (4-5 people). Ask each group to select a workplace problem that is common in the child care field, and to list ways in which they might address it individually or together. Ideally, each small group will select a different issue. Examples:

→ The isolation of working in a family child care home.

→ Finding adequate time for planning, mentoring, training or other professional activities.

→ The generally low social status and level of respect that is accorded to people who work with young children.

→ The challenge of balancing work and family responsibilities. (This is a particularly useful discussion for family child care providers, who experience a double use of their home space—for work and for family—each day.)

→ The high on-the-job exposure to childhood illnesses.

→ The physical strains of working with children—stooping, bending, lifting, sitting in child-sized rather than adult-sized chairs, etc.

→ Ways of planning a classroom environment, or of balancing a home/child-oriented environment (in terms of furniture arrangement, lighting, ventilation, storage of toys, materials and equipment, etc.) that promote relaxation and comfort, and relieve stress.

*

2. Ask the small groups then to report back to each other, and to give each other further suggestions in order to refine the "action plans" the groups have developed.

MENTORS AS LEADERS AND ADVOCATES

Designing a leadership and advocacy training component for mentors involves identifying the particular skills and knowledge which mentors will need as leaders within their workplaces and in the greater community. In this Unit we identify many of the issues that mentors will find useful as they embark upon a new professional progression: from working exclusively in the children's environment, to helping other adults put a quality program for children into effect, and, finally, to taking part in broader efforts to improve child care services for children and families and the professional status of teachers and providers.

Goals and Objectives for Unit 7

Upon completing this Unit, mentor trainees should be able to:

* discuss some of the most common obstacles which affect the quality of child care in our society;

* appreciate the ways in which they already use leadership and advocacy skills with children, parents and co-workers;

* reflect on ways to use these skills more widely in their work with adults;

* identify some of the broad range of activities in which they can participate as child care advocates and leaders; and

* understand that becoming an advocate and leader is not something beyond their reach, but rather is a learning process like any other.

The Activities in this Unit are designed to encourage mentor trainees to:

* envision their own roles in working for social change;

* discuss obstacles and shortcomings in our nation's child care delivery system;

* assess their own leadership skills;

* practice speaking out about the value of their mentoring program and/or the importance of high-quality child care;

* study other movements for social change from the past or present.

ACTIVITY 7-1

CREATING A VISION[1]

Purpose

To recognize our own ability to envision, and work toward, a better world.

Materials

Large pad of newsprint, easel and markers; paper, and pens or pencils.

Notes to Trainer

Since the point of a brainstorm (step #2) is to let one's mind work freely, no idea or suggestion should be considered unworthy. Record all responses on the flip-chart, and then let the group members decide for themselves which ones to pursue further.

Time Required

30-45 minutes.

---

[1] Thanks to Julie Olsen Edwards of Cabrillo Community College, Aptos, Calif., for suggesting this activity.

Steps for Activity 7-1

1. Ask the group select an issue in which "the world is not right" for children.

   ✳

2. Using a flip-chart to record responses, brainstorm as a group about what kinds of conditions we would need to have so that every child could fully blossom. (Presume you have all the resources you need.)

   ✳

3. After you have a list, ask each person to write down:

   → ten things from the list that could happen in 20 years;

   → then, five things from the list that could happen in five years;

   → and finally, three things they could do in the coming year to start the process of change, and the names of three possible allies who could help them.

   ✳

4. Compare and discuss these lists as a group. What are the areas of agreement and disagreement about what is possible? Do the lists suggest any ways in which the group of mentors might work together?

ACTIVITY 7-2

THE CHILD CARE DELIVERY SYSTEM AND ITS CONSEQUENCES

Purpose   To stimulate discussion about the child care staffing crisis.

Materials   Large pad of newsprint, easel and markers, as well as small sheets of paper, and pencils or pens, if you wish to take notes from the discussions, and/or ask small groups to "report back" to the larger group.

Notes to Trainer   Introduce one or more of the following topics as a springboard for *discussion* or *journal writing*.

Discussions of these questions can be held in small or large groups. If the class divides into small groups, reconvene as a large group before the session ends, to allow each small group to "report back" some of the high points of the discussion. (See also "Facilitating Discussions" on page 105.)

Alternatively, you can assign any of these questions to the mentor trainees as **journal-writing** exercises, which can then be shared or discussed later in class. (See the discussion of journal writing on page 37 of the *Handbook.*)

Time Required   20-45 minutes for each of the discussion topics, or 45-90 minutes for a session combining several of the topics.

"I was so frustrated as a preschool teacher.
I felt that nobody cared about my work, and I was planning to go back to
school so I could go into a "real" profession. Then I got involved in the
Mentor Teacher Program. It was so great to be with others who saw
themselves as professionals; it helped me to see myself that way and to realize
that child care is "for real." I want to be a better advocate so that everyone
will get a chance to experience the Mentor Program. We need more of us!
We need teachers and providers who can advocate for ourselves."

Topics for Activity 7-2

1. Why are child care wages so much lower than wages in other professions? What are the effects of these low wages—on me, on the child care profession, on children, on families, on society?

*

2. What are the obstacles, both structural and personal, to improving child care jobs? How can we overcome these obstacles? What do I need, as an individual, to be able to take action to improve child care jobs?

*

3. Sketch out a vision of quality child care—both for children and for the adults who care for them. What would really good child care look like? What would good working conditions be? How would these be different from what you now have?

*

4. How does taking action to improve child care outside the work place connect with teaching and caregiving? Does activism support or take away from your work with children?

ACTIVITY 7-3

THE JOB GAME

Purpose　To draw attention to the many skills involved in child care, and the lack of financial reward for those skills.

Materials　20-30 index cards with a different occupation written on each one. In making the cards, choose occupations that contain some aspect of child care work—such as counselor, mediator, musician, plumber, interior designer, furniture repair person, artist, athlete, fundraiser, and so on.

Notes to Trainer　While this activity alone is hardly likely to solve the problem of poor compensation in child care, it can help the mentor trainees to feel worthy of greater status and respect, which is an important stage toward assuming a new level of leadership and taking action in broader arenas.

Time Required　30-45 minutes.

Steps for Activity 7-3

1. Pass the cards around and ask each participant to choose one. Then ask:

   ➤ How many of you have an occupation card that includes some aspect of the work you do in child care?

   ➤ How many of you are holding a card for an occupation that pays less than child care? More?

   ✳

2. As a group, discuss "What's going on here and why?"—that is, "Why does a job that requires so much skill receive so little status and respect?"—since most are likely to say that this other occupation commands a higher salary than child care.

   ✳

3. Ask participants to generate a list of things that parents, directors or co-workers have done—or could do—to help them feel respected and recognized for their skills.

"I feel valued when I can help someone,
and that's why I wanted to be a mentor. Still, I feared I wouldn't be able to
go through with the program; I would be too afraid to speak publicly. But the
program has encouraged me to find the strength inside of me. It gave me a
voice. We need change, and it can't happen unless we are heard."

ACTIVITY 7-4

SPEAKING OUT FOR QUALITY CHILD CARE

Purpose   To gain practical experience in advocating for high-quality child care and professional child care careers.

Materials   Large pad of newsprint, easel and markers, for brainstorming and planning.

Notes to Trainer   Participants will need opportunities to voice their own opinions, listen to opposing viewpoints, challenge negative stereotypes, organize outreach efforts, and utilize available resources. Start with those activities that feel most comfortable, and eventually reach out to larger arenas.

Time Required   Will depend on choices below.

Options for Activity 7-4

1. Write a letter to the editor of a local newspaper, or a brief article for a child care newsletter, about the mentoring program and the opportunities it provides for new and experienced caregivers. Share personal experiences and a few well-chosen facts. Brief letters are read and printed more often. (To get started, the group can brainstorm together what the letter or article should include, and then enlist volunteers to write it.)

*

2. Hold an informational meeting for the community about the benefits gained from the mentoring program. Emphasize the personal stories, since these are what move people the most.

*

3. Develop a plan for recruiting more teachers and providers into the mentoring program.

*

4. Develop a plan for building community recognition and support for the importance of child care work.

*

5. Contact the Worthy Wage Campaign for more information on public education activities and working with the media.

ACTIVITY 7-5

LEARNING FROM OTHER SOCIAL MOVEMENTS

Purpose   To draw inspiration from other social change efforts from the past and present.

Materials   Will depend on choices below.

Notes to Trainer   To become leaders and advocates for the child care profession and for better resources for young children, mentors can benefit by looking beyond the child care world to other efforts for change. It can be very empowering to learn how other people in the past and present have made the world a better place.

Time Required   Will depend on choices below.

Options for Activity 7-5

1. Study another social change organization or coalition effort, including any that group members may have been involved in themselves. This could also be a groundbreaking movement from the past that changed how children were treated—such as the Children's Society movement for disabled children; or the fight to end child labor—or a movement to professionalize another human service field, such as nursing.

*

2. Invite a guest speaker from another such movement to come to the class to describe his or her work.

*

3. Ask each participant to identify and interview an activist in the community. Questions could include: How did the movement or action begin? How did it grow and become stronger? Why? How did leadership emerge and evolve? What might the child care movement learn from this example?

*

4. Watch a film together about a movement or an individual dealing with injustice—ranging from such documentaries as "Eyes on the Prize," "Freedom on My Mind" or "The Life and Times of Harvey Milk" to fictional stories like "Norma Rae" or "The Long Walk Home."

PLANNING A LEARNING SESSION FOR ADULTS

This Unit is designed to help mentors build on their skills of working one-to-one with other adults, by practicing ways to become effective with *groups* as public speakers, trainers and/or workshop leaders. This Unit can also give guidance to mentors who wish to form a peer support group.

As a trainer teaching this Unit, it may be helpful to recall the first workshop or training session you ever facilitated. In what areas did you feel most confident? What were your anxieties, and what helped you to overcome them? Were there any unexpected positive or negative outcomes of the experience? The answers may help you to generate ways to assist mentors as they work toward becoming public speakers, trainers or workshop leaders, and to develop resources for them as needed.

Initially, you can help mentors by reviewing their outlines and providing feedback about the appropriateness to the audience of the teaching methods they have selected, and whether the activities can be completed in the given time frame. You can also share your own experiences with mentors about preparing for and facilitating sessions, and how your skills as a trainer have changed over time.

Goals and Objectives for Unit 8

Upon completing this Unit, mentor trainees should be able to:

* understand the steps involved in *planning* a workshop, group meeting or training session;

* define and describe the main skills and methods involved in *facilitating* a group session;

* practice *implementing* a group session.

The Activities in this Unit are designed to encourage mentor trainees to:

* reflect on the factors that make a workshop or training session effective;

* practice public speaking.

ACTIVITY 8-1

IDENTIFYING GROUP SESSIONS THAT WORK

Purpose To identify the characteristics of effective group sessions by evaluating those that one has liked and disliked.

Materials Large pad of newsprint, easel and markers.

Notes to Trainer By the time we reach adulthood, we have all had many group experiences, whether in meetings, classes, at a church or synagogue, or on the job. These experiences can serve as "research data" about effective training and group methods.

Time Required 30-45 minutes.

Steps for Activity 8-1

1. Ask participants to think about a group session (meeting, training workshop, etc.) that they have enjoyed and felt contributed to their professional growth. Then, ask them to think about a group session that they did not enjoy or find useful.

   ✳

2. Share some of these experiences. What worked well, or did not work? Participants may wish to consider the following questions:

   ➤ Did you understand the purpose of the session?

   ➤ Did everyone have an opportunity to express her opinion or ask questions?

   ➤ Did participants feel pressured to express their opinions?

   ➤ How were decisions made? Did everyone understand the process?

   ➤ Did the session start and end on time?

   ➤ Did one or two people dominate the meeting?

   ➤ Did everyone understand and follow through on her responsibilities and assignments?

   ➤ Did the discussion stay on track?

   ✳

3. As a group, develop two separate lists of characteristics of productive and unproductive group sessions.

"The Mentor Program came at a critical point.
I was ready to leave the field. I felt like the Program said to me,
"You are a teacher, a professional and an advocate," and it helped me
recognize that I have those skills. I have met so many people, and so many
opportunities have opened up."

ACTIVITY 8-2

PUBLIC SPEAKING

Purpose   To provide non-threatening opportunities to practice public speaking.

Materials   Paper and pens or pencils.

Notes to Trainer   This activity gives direct feedback to participants about the importance of practice. A variation on this activity, if time permits, would be to ask participants to repeat their presentation to the same (or another) partner, after step #2, incorporating suggestions for improvement.

Time Required   30-60 minutes of class time for Steps #2 and 3. Allow at least overnight for participants to prepare their presentations.

Steps for Activity 8-2

1. Ask each participant to select a topic on which they feel very competent, and to prepare a three-to-five-minute presentation about it. The presentation can relate to child care or some aspect of their jobs, or involve another aspect of their lives, e.g., gardening, cooking or TV shows.

✳

2. In pairs or small groups of 3-4, ask participants to take turns delivering their presentations and providing feedback to each other about what was easy to understand, what was unclear, etc.

✳

3. Reconvene as a large group to discuss this experience. What did participants learn? Which types of feedback were most helpful?

FOR THE
EARLY CHILDHOOD MENTORING
CURRICULUM

Day 1: *Morning* Introduction to Mentoring (Unit 1)

Afternoon Becoming a Mentor: Options and Opportunities (Unit 2)

Day 2: Key Areas of Knowledge (Unit 3)

Morning Adult Development, and Reflective Practice

Afternoon Respecting Diversity, and the Process of Change

Day 3: *Morning* Stages of Professional Development (Unit 4)

Afternoon Building Relationships Between Mentors and Protégés (Unit 5)

Day 4: Skills for Effective Mentoring (Unit 6)

Morning Communication, Modeling, Giving and Receiving Feedback, and Observation/Coaching/Conferencing

Afternoon Self-Assessment, Resolving Conflict, and Avoiding Burnout

Day 5: *Morning* Mentors as Leaders (Unit 7)

Afternoon Training Mentors to Conduct a Learning Session for Adults (Unit 8)

Morning

Introduction to Mentoring (Unit 1)

Goals

* Gain a basic understanding of what mentoring means in the early care and education field.

* Learn why mentoring is an important development in the field.

* Identify the qualities of good mentors.

We recommend an interactive environment that engages the group of mentor trainees in developing their own lists of the qualities of good mentors (Activity 1-2) and of what mentors will be expected to do. We see Day 1 as a relatively less intensive day that will allow the trainees to get to know each other and become a cohesive group.

As a trainer, you may also wish to reflect on the discussion questions in Activity 1-1 yourself, since in some ways you will be acting as a mentor for the mentor trainees. These questions are an opportunity to reflect on your own best practices, skills, and needs for professional growth.

Afternoon

Becoming a Mentor: Options and Opportunities (Unit 2)

Goals

* Anticipate the ways in which their job descriptions and professional roles may change as a result of becoming a mentor.

* Understand the roles and responsibilities of a mentor and a protégé.

* Distinguish between mentoring and supervision.

If you are part of a formal mentoring program, this session will be your opportunity to explain program procedures as necessary, and to engage the trainees in reflecting on how best to integrate mentoring into their present jobs. The Activities are designed to get at such specifics as needs for support, and the differences between mentoring and supervision.

Key Areas of Knowledge (Unit 3)

Morning	*Afternoon*

Adult Development and Reflective Practice	**Respecting Diversity and the Process of Change**

Goals

* Understand some prominent theories of adult development, and apply them to one's own development.

* Understand the meaning and importance of reflective practice in one's work.

* Explore steps and strategies to help mentors use reflective practice in their work with protégés.

One morning is not really sufficient for covering the whole field of adult development, of course, and the mentor trainees, hopefully, will have already been exposed to some of this material. The main purpose here is to refresh them on the high points of adult development theory and to get them thinking of protégés as adult learners.

Activity 3-1 is designed to help trainees apply theories of adult development to the mentoring process, and Activity 3-2 introduces journal writing as a tool to foster reflective practice in one's daily work.

Goals

* Understand some of the goals and principles of culturally relevant anti-bias education, particularly as they apply to relationships between mentors and protégés.

* Review material about the process of change in individuals and organizations, as it may relate to the mentoring program's impact on child care classrooms and homes.

Talking about diversity and bias inevitably includes reflecting on one's own experiences, attitudes and practices. Activities 3-3 to 3-6 are designed to foster constructive, challenging dialogue and reflection about ourselves, as well as practical experience in addressing our daily practices in the classroom or family child care home.

Our material on the change process is intended to help trainees understand the benefits of change, even when it is a slow and difficult process, and to think about ways of implementing change thoughtfully and supportively. Activity 3-7 can help trainees reflect on some of their own experiences of personal change.

Morning

Stages of Professional Development (Unit 4)

Goals

✳ Familiarize oneself with Lilian Katz's theory of preschool teacher development, and with the most commonly identified needs of beginning teachers and providers.

✳ Be able to assess one's own and one's protégé's stages of development, in order to better assess priority areas for learning and growth during the mentoring relationship.

Activities 4-1 and 4-2 are designed to help mentor trainees assess their own developmental stages as teachers or providers, and to classify some of the specific behaviors they might see in their protégés along a continuum of development. The discussion questions in Activity 4-3 can help boost mentors' self-awareness about the experiences, people and events that have contributed to their professional growth.

Afternoon

Building Relationships Between Mentors and Protégés (Unit 5)

Goals

✳ Identify program structures necessary to support mentoring (e.g. time and space to meet).

✳ Clarify expectations for the mentoring relationship.

✳ Understand the stages which the mentor/ protégé relationship might undergo.

This session is an opportunity to discuss such nuts-and-bolts issues as when and where mentors and protégés will meet, classroom/ home coverage, and helping mentor/protégé relationships get off on the right foot. The Activities are geared to helping mentors reflect on these issues, and on their own expectations and needs.

Skills for Effective Mentoring (Unit 6)

Morning

Communication, Modeling, Giving and Receiving Feedback, and Observation/Coaching/Conferencing

Goals

* Review communication skills, and practice the art of active listening.

* Understand the importance of modeling as an adult education practice.

* Consider ways to create a climate in which suggestions for change or improvement are offered supportively.

* Familiarize oneself with methods of observation, coaching and conferencing; e.g., how to "ask the right questions."

Afternoon

Self-Assessment, Resolving Conflict, and Avoiding Burnout

Goals

* Familiarize oneself with self-assessment/self-evaluation instruments that can be used by mentors and protégés.

* Review models of positive conflict resolution.

* Understand the symptoms and causes of, and solutions to, burnout in the early care and education field.

By this stage of the training, we are zeroing in on the areas of skill that mentors will be expected to develop in their work with protégés. While this will be a full day, covering a lot of important material, it is also more practical and less theoretical than some of the previous sessions. We have designed the Activities to be practical opportunities to try out these areas of skill—for example, Activity 6-1, "Active Listening," and the role plays on resolving conflict in Activity 6-3.

Morning

Mentors as Leaders (Unit 7)

Goals

* Define leadership in the context of early care and education.

* Identify the range of activities and situations in which mentors can exhibit and practice leadership.

* Examine some of the major structural problems and challenges in the current U.S. child care delivery system.

* Understand the leadership roles that mentors can play, in improving services for children and work environments for teachers and providers.

This session will give mentors the opportunity to explore their understanding of leadership and advocacy as it applies to the child care field as a whole. The Appendices and lists of further reading in the *Handbook* will provide mentors with background information, but the Activities are focused primarily on recognizing one's own ability to envision social change and take action, and on building leadership skills.

Afternoon

Training Mentors to Conduct a Learning Session for Adults (Unit 8)

Goals

* Be able to apply principles of adult learning to the planning of *group* learning situations.

* Understand the steps involved in planning and conducting an effective learning session for a group of adults.

* Improve skills in facilitating group processes.

This Unit is designed to help the trainees look ahead to opportunities to work as mentors or trainers with *groups* of protégés or other adults. The Activities are designed to help the mentor trainees reflect on the factors that make a workshop or training session effective, and to practice public speaking.

Depending on the composition and needs of particular groups, however, some trainers might choose not to include this Unit in their mentoring course. Instead, one might spend an extra session (e.g., the morning of Day 5) on the mentoring skills covered in Unit 6, and then complete the course with an afternoon session on Unit 7, "Mentors as Leaders."

1. Introductions

Introductory activities can range from simply going around the room and saying names, to posing more involved warm-up questions for people to answer about their program or reasons for coming to the session. Sometimes it's a good icebreaker to ask participants to share something they like to do outside of work. If there are lots of people, you might consider introductions or warm-up activities in smaller groups or pairs. Sometimes even a show of hands in response to a question (e.g., how many of you have ever led a circle time with children before?) can make people feel they are joining with others with similar concerns or skills.

First impressions about a meeting or session go a long way in shaping feelings about the experience. Among the issues to consider are:

* Is everyone personally greeted when they enter the session?

* Are name tags available if everyone does not know each other?

* Beyond a hello, does everyone have information about the agenda—either receiving their own copy or shown where it is written for all to see?

* Has time been allotted to review the agenda? Sessions work best when people share an understanding of why they have come together and what they will be doing.

* Is there a plan if activities take longer than expected? It's helpful for the trainer, or the trainer and the participants, to prioritize agenda items so that additional time isn't lost deciding what to cover and what to skip.

2. Facilitating Discussions

To facilitate something is to make it run smoothly. A facilitator:

* starts the meeting

* calls upon people during discussions

* helps people to clarify what they mean and to stay on the topic

* keeps track of time

* moves the group through its agenda.

Co-facilitating is another helpful way for new (and experienced) leaders to share responsibility. In the thick of things, it is easy to get a little off track. If two people are facilitating, one can keep track of time and assess the emotional tenor of the group, while another focuses on moving through the agenda.

The following are some of the skills that will assist mentors in guiding discussions:

listening

gatekeeping

supporting

clarifying

harmonizing

summarizing

relieving tension

sharing information

evaluating

appreciating/encouraging

maintaining focus

"Gatekeeping," for example, means keeping the channel of communication open to all participants, making sure that everyone gets a chance to talk, and intervening or redirecting whenever anyone interrupts or rambles. As a gatekeeper, a trainer might say, for example, "Joan, I see you have something to say over there," or "Eleanor, I think you're discussing a different topic, which we'll get to later."

All of these skills are necessary for a group to run smoothly but they don't need to be embodied in just one person. Many of the training participants have some of these skills, and can also be encouraged to use them during the session.

3. Tools for Effective Facilitation[1]

"Reading the group" accurately is a skill that can significantly enhance the rapport between you and your participants. Anticipating basic needs is the first step in this process. For example, plan for breaks if your session is lengthy, and provide food, comfortable chairs, adequate lighting and a comfortable room temperature. Be prepared to address a variety of learning styles. Also allow participants adequate "wait" time; it may often take them five seconds or more to process a question, or synthesize the ideas on the table, before they are ready to respond. This extra gift of "thinking time" is an effective strategy in soliciting optimal group involvement. Be familiar, also, with group dynamics. Be aware of "group think," an excessive tendency to maintain "group cohe-

---

[1] Adapted, with permission, from Newton et al. (1994). "Tools for Effective Facilitation," 1-165 to 1-169.

siveness" at the cost of critical thinking and risk taking. Remember the significance of silence as a voice of the group. In cases in which silence is "spoken loudly," you may want to ask the question, "Does anyone have any thought, question or concern they would like to put on the table at this point?"

Clarifying what someone has said is helpful to ensure common understanding and decrease the possibility of unnecessary conflict. Paraphrasing or checking for accuracy can help participants clarify their intentions and let them know that you hear them accurately.

Probing for specificity is a skill that facilitators can employ to help move individuals, or groups, from a position of "feeling stuck" to one of new understanding or enlightenment. By asking certain kinds of questions, a facilitator can coach a reflective process that often invites discovery and clarity. Examples of this type of question would include:

* What would that look like?

* How is what you've just said different from this other idea?

* Could you expand that further?

Depersonalizing conflict is essential in order to be an impartial facilitator. When working with diverse groups, the personality, tone or learning style needs of participants may cloud your perceptions and attitudes as the facilitator. It is essential that you focus on the problem, not the person, when responding to difficult issues in facilitating groups. At the same time, it is often necessary to give difficult feedback. For instance, if group behaviors like blocking, sabotaging, excessive humor or monopolizing are occurring, you may need to step into the role of process observer and provide the group with specific data that identifies the unproductive behavior. If you are "stepping out" of your facilitator role for any reason, it is important to announce what you are doing and why, i.e., you may shift to a process observer role to provide the group with needed feedback. In any case, always attempt to remove your own ego from the conflict. As facilitator, you need to remain impartial in resolving controversy.

Bracketing is a technique that allows questions, comments, and ideas to be validated while at the same time allowing the group to move forward. For example, if an issue is raised that is important to the group, yet unrelated to its present task, you could record the issue or topic on newsprint, place it within brackets { } and indicate that this is an important issue the group may have to return to at a later time. It is also important to include bracketed information in the minutes. This technique provides you with one way to keep a group on task, while inviting a disposition for critical inquiry.

Valuing each person's contributions will enhance group development by giving personal meaning to each member's participation. There are several ways you may do this:

* Give a person positive feedback for a comment; for example, "That's a really good suggestion."

* Bring back into the conversation a comment made previously that would otherwise be overlooked. It is also helpful if, in doing so, you are able to make connections to the current conversation.

* Provide a visual focus point for the meeting's progress. Newsprint is a wonderful facilitation tool in this regard. Not only will it allow participants to see what they have talked about, but it is also a good way to review decisions that have already been made.

* Check with participants to make sure that what you record on newsprint accurately reflects what they said. Try to use the exact language or phrases used by participants as much as possible.

Be Prepared

It is a good idea to have a "tool kit" prepared and to take it with you whenever you facilitate a group session. Regardless of what others have agreed to prepare for you, Murphy's Law often rings true when it comes to having exactly what you need on any given occasion. Helpful tools to include in your facilitator kit are:

a variety of colored markers

overhead pens

masking tape

timer or stopwatch

pushpins

paper clips

name tags

rubber bands

post-it notes

business cards

portable easel

large pad of newsprint

audiotape recorder

A Framework for Effective Meetings

* Have an agenda, or "build" one at the beginning of the session.

* Record highlights, decisions and bracketed information on newsprint and use this information to create a set of minutes of the session.

* Provide a copy of the minutes to each participant.

* Be prepared to change your facilitator role to one of process observer if feedback is needed regarding group behavior.

* Provide participants with an opportunity to give you feedback about their experience during the session.

4. Dealing with Difficult Dynamics

Group work is challenging, even under the best of circumstances. Here are some typical problems that may emerge during sessions:

* Participants are doing distracting things, such as having separate conversations on the side.

* People come late, leave early, or walk in and out of the session.

* Someone is dominating the discussion.

* Some participants rarely or never join in the discussion.

* Participants are becoming tense with each other.

* Strong opinions or feelings are preventing constructive discussion.

* People are discussing many issues at once.

In each of these situations, the first task will be to determine what is at issue for those involved. If participants are doing distracting things, such as sending notes to another person or walking in and out, their behavior may signal that they are not interested in or identified with what is going on. Next, brainstorm what can be done to prevent these situations. Maybe the particular discussion does not really need to involve the whole group, for example, and that is why it is not holding everyone's attention. Or maybe everyone needs a break. A facilitator can ask people directly what they need in order to feel more involved in the process or can call a break and discuss the issue privately with the people concerned.

It is important to be conscious of power relationships within the group. Because of the diversity in age, ethnicity, class and other experiences among those who work with young children, expect to find real differences among people with respect to self-confidence and skills. Unknowingly, because of past educational and other experiences, some participants may move faster than others, preventing some from contributing to discussion. Take time to notice who is participating and engaged in the group. If only the European-Americans, the men or the center-based staff are speaking up, it will be necessary for the group to explore why people of color, women or family child care providers feel less involved.

5. Decision Making

Depending on the topic and structure of the session, there may be issues that you as the leader will want the group to decide as a whole. What process will be used to come to decisions? Will you strive for consensus (agreement by all participants) on all decisions, or will you abide by a majority vote when not everyone can agree?

When a group is coming to a decision, the leader or facilitator plays a critical role. You can point out areas of agreement and clarify where the real differences lie. (For example, "We all agreed that we want to focus on gross motor activities, but we haven't decided whether we want to start with outdoor or indoor curriculum.") It is important when coming to a decision that all members participate. A facilitator mustn't assume that silence means agreement in a group. Be sure that everyone expresses an opinion when a decision is being made.

Approaches to Decision Making[2]

Individuals are more likely to support a decision in which they have played a part—a factor that underscores the importance of the entire problem-solving process. Although it is often difficult to achieve an agreed-upon decision (because group members lean heavily toward the solutions they propose), it is crucial for participants to realize that avoiding a decision is, in fact, a decision—a choice *not* to move forward or change the status quo. Sound decisions are precursors to productive action—the crux of effective change.

---

[2] Adapted with permission of the authors from *Assisting Change in Education (ACE): A Training Program for School Improvement Facilitators, Trainers' Manual,* by E.R. Saxl, with M.B. Miles and A. Lieberman. (1989), Appendix I-E.

Mentor trainers can help groups make decisions in several ways. Group decisions are sometimes made by individuals or subgroups who push through a decision, relying on the passivity of the other participants. This is particularly likely to happen when a group begins meeting and informal leaders take charge of the decision-making process. Trainers can confront that pattern of decision making by commenting on its frequency and questioning whether all opinions are being taken into consideration.

Decision-making methods include:

* *Majority vote.* More than half the group members agree on a single choice. A major drawback is that those who voted against the decision may not be committed to its implementation.

* *Unanimous vote.* All group members agree. Problems may arise because some people who feel the pressure to agree may not really support the decision, and because one person can block the decision by disagreeing.

* *Consensus.* Internal discussion and polls take place to find common points of agreement. In the course of trying to reach consensus, group members suggest modi-

fications to the original proposal that may be acceptable to others, resulting in a genuine agreement to implement the revised decision. This method, although time-consuming, is most appropriate when important policy decisions are being made.

Many believe that decisions made by consensus are of higher quality than those arrived at through other forms of decision-making. Consensus is a collective opinion arrived at by a group whose members have listed carefully to the opinions of others, have communicated openly, and have been able to state their opposition to other members' views and seek alternatives in a constructive manner. When a decision is made by consensus, all members—because they have had the opportunity to influence it—should feel they understand the decision and can support it.

Johnson and Johnson (1975) provide the following guidelines for consensual decision making:

* Avoid blindly arguing for your own individual judgments. Present your position as clearly and logically as possible, but listen to other members' reactions and consider them carefully before you press your point.

* Avoid changing your mind *only* to reach agreement and avoid conflict. Support only solutions to which you are at least somewhat agreeable. Yield only to positions that have an objective and logically sound foundation.

* Avoid "conflict-reducing" procedures such as majority vote, tossing a coin, averaging or bargaining in reaching decisions.

* Seek out differences of opinion; they are natural and expected. Try to involve everyone in the decision process. Disagreements can help the group's decision because they present a wide range of information and opinions, thereby creating a better chance for the group to hit upon more adequate solutions.

* Do not assume that someone must win and someone must lose when discussion reaches a stalemate. Instead, look for the next most acceptable alternative for all members.

* Discuss underlying assumptions, listen carefully to one another, and encourage the participation of all members.

6. Types of Evaluation Methods

Written Scale

This method of assessment provides a numerical evaluation of a session. Typically, participants rate the session around several areas on a scale of one to five. For example:

Today's session was:

Not productive	I	2	3	4	5	Very productive

Not well-organized	I	2	3	4	5	Very well-organized

Open-ended assessment

This provides for more information and is especially useful if you are working with a particular group over time. The responses can help inform what a particular group of learners will need next, and will provide the trainer with feedback about whether or not their expectations were met. The following statements can be placed in the top of each of four quadrants of a 8.5x11 piece of paper.

I came expecting . . .	I got . . .
I value . . .	Next I need . . .

Quick written or non-verbal feedback

There are two methods that can provide quick access to participants' assessment of a workshop, a reading assignment, or other training process. Immediately following the activity, ask participants to give you a thumbs-up if they thought the activity was very interesting or helpful; a thumbs-down if they did not find it useful or engaging; and a thumbs-parallel if they are neutral about the activity. A second method is to ask participants to record on 3" x 5" cards one thing they liked and one suggestion for improvement.

Straightforward discussion

This is often the most direct and effective form of evaluation, and it provides an added opportunity to talk about the process of the session, not just the content. Basically, the facilitator asks for the following information:

* What did you like about the session? What worked well for you? What do you feel you learned?

* What did you dislike about the session? What didn't work well?

* What would you change in the next session to address any concerns you've identified?

People often avoid this method because they are not comfortable with raising concerns. Mentors can help to model positive ways to share concerns with other adults. The key is for participants to say why something didn't work for them, and then to suggest an alternative—essentially the same approach that adults use with children. Consider how different it feels to hear, "Mary let Sue dominate the meeting," compared to, "When one person talks a lot, it's hard for me to break into the discussion. It would help if you make sure that other people have spoken before calling on the same person a second time."

7. Parting Thoughts

* Be prepared.

* Know your audience.

* Embrace participants' ideas and interests.

* Use appropriate tone of voice and body language. It has been estimated that over half of your message depends on body language, one-third on tone of voice, and less than ten percent on the words you choose.

* Celebrate the unexpected.

* Demonstrate a sense of humor—have fun!

Like working with children, working with adults is a continual learning process. *The Early Childhood Mentoring Curriculum* has been designed as a beginning course, with the understanding that trainees will need ongoing mentoring themselves in order to become better and better mentors as time goes on—either in an ongoing mentor support group, or by receiving continuing training.

This concluding section includes two "wrap-up" training activities: one for the end of the mentoring course ("Hopes and Fears: A Letter to Myself"), and one for the end of the mentoring year or program period ("Program Evaluation").

We hope that this Curriculum has been a useful starting place for your mentor training program, to which mentors can turn again and again over the course of their professional development.

ACTIVITY C-I

HOPES AND FEARS: A LETTER TO MYSELF[1]

Purpose To help new mentors set appropriate goals for their work with protégés. This activity is designed to help anticipate success and to express any concerns about the responsibility of mentoring that new mentors are about to undertake.

Materials Paper, pens or pencils, and envelopes.

Notes to Trainer This activity will be most effective if done after the initial mentor training, and close to the time when mentors have been matched with protégés. The letters are meant to be personal and private—but their contents can be a powerful source of reflection at the end of the year if mentors choose to share them.

Time Required 20-30 minutes initially; undetermined for follow-up.

---

[1] Adapted, with permission, from Newton et al. (1994).

Steps for Activity C-1

1. Ask mentors to write a letter to themselves addressing the following questions:

   → What do you hope for yourself and the person(s) you will be mentoring in the coming months?

   → What concerns and fears do you have as you embark on this experience?

   *

2. Ask mentors to place their letter in an envelope, seal it and address it to themselves. Collect the envelopes.

   *

3. Prior to the end of the mentoring program, deliver these letters back to their owners. Ask mentors to voluntarily share a portion of their letters with other mentors, focusing on:

   → Whether their hopes and/or fears were realized.

   → How the training, their match with their protégé and other components of the program affected their hopes and fears.

ACTIVITY C-2

PROGRAM EVALUATION

Purpose To provide the mentoring program with helpful feedback from the participants' points of view.

Materials Sufficient copies of the evaluation questionnaires for mentors and protégés (Appendices 6 and 7 of the *Handbook*).

Notes to Trainer Indicate to mentors and protégés that these questionnaires will be kept confidential, and that they may complete them anonymously if they prefer. You may also wish to adapt the questionnaires to your own needs, depending on the types of evaluation data and feedback your program would like to collect.

Time Required 20-30 minutes if completed during a class or group session.

Steps for Activity C-2

1. Distribute copies of the questionnaires to mentors and protégés.

    *

2. Either collect the completed questionnaires during a group session, or set a deadline by which they should be returned.

References

Council on Interracial Books for Children, and Multicultural Project for Communication and Education. (1984). *Child Care Shapes the Future: Anti-Racist Strategies* (filmstrip). New York: CIBC.

Derman-Sparks, L., and the ABC Task Force (1989). *Anti-Bias Curriculum.* Washington, DC: National Association for the Education of Young Children.

Gilligan, C., Ward, J.V., and Taylor, L., with Bardige, B. (1988). *Mapping the Moral Domain.* Cambridge: Harvard University Press.

Guidice, A. and Wortis, S., eds. (1987). *Cultural Links: A Multicultural Resource Guide.* Cambridge, MA: Multicultural Project for Communication and Education (out of print).

Hidalgo, N. (1993). "Multicultural Teacher Introspection." In T. Perry and J. Fraser, eds., *Freedom's Plow.* New York: Routledge.

Johnson, D.W., and Johnson, F.P. (1975). *Joining Together: Group Theory and Group Skills.* Englewood Cliffs, NJ: Prentice-Hall.

Killion, J.P. (1990). "The Benefits of An Induction Program for Experienced Teachers." *Journal of Staff Development.*

Levine, S.L. (1989). *Promoting Adult Growth in Schools: The Promise of Professional Development.* Boston: Allyn and Bacon.

Lieberman, A. and Miller, L., eds. (1991). *Staff Development for Education in the '90s: New Demands, New Realities, New Perspectives.* Second Edition. New York: Teachers College Press.

Newton, A., Bergstrom, K., Brennan, N., Dunne, K., Gilbert, C., Ibarguen, N., Perez-Selles, M., and Thomas, E. (1994). *Mentoring: A Resource and Training Guide for Educators.* Andover, MA: The Regional Laboratory for Educational Improvement.

Odell, S.J. (1990). *Mentor Teacher Programs.* Washington, D.C.: National Education Association.

Sahier, J. and Gowner, R. (1987). *The Skillful Teacher: Building Your Teaching Skills.* Carlisle, MA: Research for Better Teaching.

Whitebook, M., and Sakai, L. (1995). *The Potential of Mentoring: An Assessment of the California Early Childhood Mentor Program.* Washington, D.C.: Center for the Child Care Workforce.

Mentoring in Early Care and Education: Refining an Emerging Career Path, by Marcy Whitebook, Patty Hnatiuk and Dan Bellm (1994).

A resource book based on the varied experiences of mentor programs across the country, as reported during a national Mentoring Roundtable held in June 1994. Highlights critical issues in developing mentor programs and in helping them become well-established in one's community.

The Potential of Mentoring: An Assessment of the California Early Childhood Mentor Program, by Marcy Whitebook and Laura Sakai (1995).

A wide-ranging examination of the largest early childhood mentoring program in the United States. Focuses on mentors' and protégés' own assessment of the program, and compares the mentoring field-practicum experience with lab school classrooms.

Early Childhood Mentoring Programs: A Survey of Community Initiatives, by Gretchen Stahr Breunig and Dan Bellm (1996).

In-depth profiles of 19 mentoring programs throughout the country, covering such issues as program design, recruitment and selection of mentors and protégés, training, compensation, funding, evaluation, obstacles and successes.